SERMONS FOR
THE GREAT DAYS
OF THE YEAR

REV. RUSSELL H. CONWELL, D.D.

SERMONS FOR THE GREAT DAYS OF THE YEAR

BY

REV. RUSSELL H. CONWELL, D.D.

MINISTER AT THE TEMPLE, PHILADELPHIA

Author of "Acres of Diamonds," etc.

NEW YORK
GEORGE H. DORAN COMPANY

PRINTED IN THE UNITED STATES OF AMERICA

CONTENTS

v

PAGE

SERMONS
FOR THE GREAT DAYS
OF THE YEAR

I

New Year and Debt

(ROMANS XIII:7)

I WILL make up in briefness what I lack in illustration in order that you may not go into the
New Year without the lesson I had in mind to leave.

It is time that we were thinking of the first of
January, and so to-night, I turn your attention to the
13th chapter of Romans, and the 7th verse:

*"Render therefore to all their dues; tribute to
whom tribute is due, custom to whom custom, fear
to whom fear, honor to whom honor."*

"Owe no man anything, but to love one another."

Any one who sleeps overnight with money in his
pocket which is overdue to some one else, is a thief.
May I repeat that sentence: "ANY ONE WHO SLEEPS

9

OVER NIGHT WITH MONEY IN HIS POCKET WHICH
IS DUE TO SOME ONE ELSE IS A THIEF."

Again, any man who makes an unnecessary present
on Christmas when he owes an honest debt, is also
a thief. I need not repeat that, because we all see
it the first time.

In the Bible, in setting forth the character of the
Christians of the early Church at a time when it
was necessary especially that men should clearly represent the truth, it was set forth very distinctly:
"Owe no man anything, but to love one another."

At the end of the year we generally take an account of stock, to find out whether we owe or do
not, and it is necessary for a man who would live
rightly with himself, his family, his neighbors and
his God, that he should frequently take very careful
account, and especially at this, the end of the year.

"Owe no man anything." I may explain what
perhaps is clear to most of you, that when the Bible
exhorts us to "owe no man anything," it does not
say you should not have a mortgage on your house;
it does not say you should not give a note; it does
not say that you should not borrow money. It is the
extremist who interprets things in that way. No
man "owes" anything that isn't due, in a moral or
religious sense. That is the true interpretation. No
man can be said to owe anything which is not yet
due. You are under no moral obligation to pay a

man a note six months before it is due, but the day it becomes due you owe it, and this it is that the Bible says we must not owe any man; it means that we must not have any overdue notes, any overdue promises, any unfulfilled pledges, which should have been paid the day before.

"Owe no man anything" is as distinct a command of God as any of the Ten Commandments, and life becomes a continually harassing thing to a person who does owe. Any man or woman who owes what he cannot pay is in slavery; we all know that, and he who runs in debt without seeing that he is able to pay it when it comes due, comes under the condemnation of God, so that he may be declared a thief. It is stealing, pure and simple, only by a roundabout method. So I need not enforce that thought, as I think we all understand that the Lord commands every disciple of His to keep out of debt, to keep out of that position where he owes anything that he cannot pay.

I have often been asked by friends if I believed that the curse of God really rested upon people who had committed some unpardonable sin, and it is too wide a subject and too deep for me to explain, and yet I have a very strong inclination to believe that under certain circumstances God does let His curse descend upon men, and that it remaineth with them ever after they have committed some terrible sin; and one of the greatest sins is not to pay what a man owes, and to pay it at the time he agreed to pay it. It is not enough, in God's sight, to pay a debt to-morrow that is due to-day, or to go to bank the day after to meet a note that was due the day before.

In order to set before the world an example that should bring it to Christ, the Apostle saw very clearly the need in that church, in the very beginning of the Church of Christ, for him to lay down this irrevocable law: "Thou shalt owe no man anything," and if a man does run in debt, he certainly comes under the curse, in a sense, of the living God.

But I cannot say that curse is something that remaineth forever over a man, and I am sure it may not. For if he repents sincerely and will turn unto the Lord, he will, of course, be forgiven. But I remember a personal incident which illustrates this point. I was working for $15 a week. I had a wife and two children. My pay came to me every Saturday at one o'clock. I know what it is for a working man to go around at one o'clock to get his pay; I know what it is for him to go to the window for his envelope, and to take out the money which he has counted upon all week, and which his wife has carefully estimated upon until they know where every penny of it is to go. These simple incidents come into every one of your lives, or else I would not allude to this. One day father and mother told us they wanted to have son and wife and grand-children come home over a Sunday, and as the Monday following was a holiday, it would give them two days at home. Our home was some distance from the great city, and so the young man, and his wife, and the two children talked over their visit to grand-father and grandmother—they had not seen them for a long time, and the grandmother had not seen one of the children at all. So they decided that they would go the next Saturday, at the close of the week's work, which ended at twelve o'clock, and take the train leaving at 2:30; and thus go into the country and visit the old folks. They had written weeks before that they were coming, grandfather had ar-ranged that a team should come to the station—everything was arranged, just as you have done it many times. The children were carefully dressed, and lunch was put up, for we could not afford to buy any on the way, and my wife and the two chil-dren went to the station. I went about my duties in the morning after breakfast, and I had told them that I would meet them at the station at two o'clock. I went around to the paying office at one o'clock as usual, and the clerk was not in. He was out to a baseball game, but they said he would "be back pretty soon." Being a relative of the proprietor, he could do some things that others could not. So I sat around that office till the train went out, and burst into tears. There was no other train that day but one that would get us there late in the night, or perhaps the next morning. But he did not come at all, and I walked down to the railroad station and told my broken-hearted wife that we could not go. I had not the money to buy a ticket, and did not know any friends that I could borrow it from, so we turned back, walked up those desolate streets, and ate our cold lunch in the tenement where we lived, and all the next day and the following holiday was a funeral to us. We could not go, we did not go, and there is hardly a sadder chapter in the life of that poor old man's heart to-night than to think how his wife and children, and father and mother, were disappointed because the bookkeeper did not pay those wages at the time they should have been paid. He did not pay the debts that should have been paid at the time he should have paid them. I did not wish him any harm. But I left the employ of that company, in the Providence of God: or I would not have been here.

Every commandment of God has attached to it a promise, and a punishment, and he who breaks it, and breaks it ruthlessly for selfish purposes, seems to come under some visitation of the curse of God; good fortune never comes his way; hard luck is always his experience, and there is nothing in human life that brings so much general sorrow as

the failure of man to pay his honest debts. The
Bible here declared distinctly that thou shalt render
"tribute to whom tribute" is due. Oh, what a far-
reaching command that was, when you think of the
people of the East, under the terrible Roman Government, compelled by taxation to pay so large a
share of maintaining that great military system of
that day! When we find that Apostle telling them
that they must pay that tribute, which to a great
extent was unjust, he is going a long distance, and
my mind hesitates, my conscience trembles on the
verge of advice like that. If I were, like the Jew,
under tribute to the Roman Government which had
held my nation by mere military force, I question
whether I would be following Christ with fullness
of heart, and pay cheerfully the taxes they de-
manded of me. That is an extreme line, and when
the Apostle goes so far as to declare that they
ought even to pay that tribute, then he sweeps everything; there can be nothing beyond that demand.
He also said, "You are to pay your custom house
all that is due." What a universal thing it is for
people coming from other countries to try to escape
the custom-house duties. But they never make anything by it; they always lose, because God sets the
current of His Providence against them, and while
nothing seems to be open or distinct, yet by placing
themselves in a position of defrauding the Govern-

ment, they have placed themselves in such a relation with the nation, and with themselves, that they are ever out of accord, never in the right place at the right time. So the Bible declares that it is our duty to pay customs, so long as the Government of the land lays a tax upon goods brought in.

Then it goes on to say that you must not owe any man anything; you must pay your taxes. But there are often men who think they are honest and upright, who would escape, if possible, the payment of their share of the expenses of the city, or of the State, in the payment for sidewalks, streets, or the protection of the police for their comfort—they would not pay what was their due.

This disposition is sometimes found in a Christian church.

There lived at Avon, N. Y., two of the noblest Christian men it has ever been my good fortune to meet. One of those two men died last week at Avon, and I had never known their inside history before. But Mr. Puffer and his brother-in-law went into partnership forty-one years ago. They bought a farm and they went to raising cattle, and selling certified milk for invalids and infants, and those two men lived together for forty-one years, until Mr. Puffer died last week, without a separate account—all having the same pocketbook for forty-one years. They dealt in large things; they ran great enterprises, and each one brought up his own family, and I sat last week in the parlor of that great mansion, at each end of which lived the families of these people, and neither of them had a separate bank account. I felt the sublimity of the situation. They had great enterprises in Europe; they had factories in Germany; one of the men most prominent in Western New York, the other still living, Mr. Markham, is one of the grand old men of that State. The ministration of the children is sweet to behold. I believe they told me that those two men never had a single angry word with each other, and the families lived with each other with all that sweetness, with no quarrel ever having come up to separate them. Before the wife of one of them died a few years ago, she said to me: "Pray that I may live; I am not afraid to die; I love God and I believe in Jesus Christ, and He has forgiven my sins. But I want to live on for my husband's sake. He has been so kind to me. Oh," she said, "I feel so grateful to God for my husband, and I cannot bear to let him want for any ministrations that I could give him. I feel that God has been so merciful to me in giving him to me that I could hardly ask for more. But I do want you to pray that I may live on to minister to him, for his great goodness to me." When the ideal of this commandment is carried out, and we appreciate our obligations to our fellowmen to the full, then there will arise that respect for God and love for each other that makes life so beautiful, and brings heaven indeed to earth. How strong is the man who realizes his obligations!

Once I visited the little kingdom of Montenegro, which now stands again as the key of Europe. That brave little kingdom of Montenegro! Germany with her great army conquered Servia and has come up to the rocks and valleys and hills of little Montenegro! Even so came Napoleon with his conquering army; coming from splendid victories, believing that he would sweep the east, hoping to go even to Babylon, with his great army, numbering more than that German army. Like the German Emperor, he had been training his army for many years, yet when Napoleon came up to the rocks of Montenegro— "Thus far shalt thou go," said the God of battles, "and no further," and he was obliged to retreat before the little kingdom, not half the size of Pennsylvania. Many a battle has been fought there since, and they have come up to Montenegro again and again. Only ten years since the Turk came up there, but they were compelled to stop. Montenegro has no great castles; Montenegro has no great fortresses; Montenegro has no 15-inch guns. Oh, no! But when the victorious army of the German tyrant, with all their wealth of forty years of discipline, came up to the foot of the mountains of Montenegro, the newspapers said yesterday "they had stopped there."

As we think of "preparedness" in this country, we must remember that the best preparedness on earth is the preparation of brains and heart, which is worth more than guns. Yes, though we might need them, without heart patriotism working together, love of country, brotherhood among ourselves, we will be worth nothing, even though we have a larger navy and a mighty army. Little Montenegro! Watch that kingdom! They love each other; they are brothers indeed. I visited that capital of that little kingdom, and everywhere courtesy of those mountaineers tor each other, and kindness toward their friends and their children, the sense of obligation to take better care of their friends' orphans, than they would of their own children, made it a place inspiring to visit, and filled us full of esteem, and you felt humanity was higher and grander there in those mountains, underneath those snowy peaks than anywhere else on the face of the earth. The Montenegran believes that God has given him that country; thanks God for that country, and he believes he is under obligation to his fellowmen for continual assistance. Those mighty snow storms, as they send their awful avalanches down the mountain sides, bring often distress and suffering to those people, but they help each other and as the poor people are more helpful to each other than the rich ever are, so the Montenegrans love each other, and are interested in each other's happiness and in each other's home. While they have their schools and their churches and are a very progressive, intelligent people, and the queen of Italy is the daughter of the king of that little country, they do love each other, and their thanksgivings are continual. I went into their cathedral, in that capital city, and the songs they sang, the bright, happy faces that I looked upon as they praised God were so in contrast with what I had seen across the water that I could not help but mark it. They love their country, and they feel indebted to each other, and feeling that indebtedness makes them magnificent specimens of heroes, of patriots, and of real Christians. I believe that the great tide of war will break again on the foot of the rocks of Montenegro, because those brave men stand so together like those that stood at Thermopylæ.

The time has come when we are at the end of the year, and we will come to take an account of ourselves with God. Let us remember when the first of January comes around that we owe much to God for all the blessings that He has given us through the year, for friends who have been raised up for us; for opportunity to do what Christ taught us to do; for health and strength and education, and for the fact that God has given us Jesus Christ as a propitiation for our sins.

Let us take a very careful account of ourselves at the end of this year, and feel deeply, sincerely, our obligation to God, and don't let the first of January come until we have paid our debt, or secured its payment through Jesus Christ.

Let not the sun go down on any debt that you can pay, and let not the New Year come on with any bill unpaid which you can pay, and with all things, pay your debt to God; pay it with humility, pay it with repentance, pay it with prayer, pay it with love for God and love for mankind, and begin the New Year square with mankind and square with God.

St. Valentine's Marriage Reform

IN the story of the wise and foolish virgins which I read this evening, in the 25th chapter and the 1st verse, Jesus said:

"Then shall the kingdom of heaven be likened unto ten virgins, which took their lamps, and went forth to meet the bridegroom."

It is Jesus' description of a wedding. You will notice in all the history of the Saviour's life on earth His references to anything were ever to those of the very highest type. His thoughts were pure as the light from the sun, and the illustrations which He used were in themselves helpful and inspiring in every possible direction.

It was a wonderful parable; though I am not here to speak of the parable or its story, but simply of one of its suggestions. Of all the characters in forms of beauty, of all that has been condensed into a few expressions of wisdom or poetry, of the marvelous and the majestic, there is found nothing finer, nothing more eloquent than Jesus' reference to a wedding. He refers to it as being an institution in which His Heavenly Father is interested, in which He Himself has taken such especial interest that He allowed it to be put on record that the first miracle He ever performed was in the turning of water into wine at a wedding in Galilee. His reverence for the marriage ties, His references to home and childhood, and to all the associated domestic loveliness which gathers around a dwelling where love is, are full of that spirit which lifts the heart unto God. Wonderful, wonderful Saviour of mankind!

He says that there was a marriage feast, and that ten virgins were invited, and five were admitted and five kept out. He uses marriage, its occasion, its ceremonies, and its sacredness to enforce His important theological thought. Why was my attention called to it this evening? Because yesterday was St. Valentine's Day. While this generation seem to have forgotten the purposes for which St. Valentine's Day was first celebrated, it is an occasion that calls attention to the marriage of men and women, to home life and child life, and to all the domestic felicities that are connected with such relationships. St. Valentine's Day has become an occasion when people send ludicrous pictures from one to another or try to surprise each other with some anonymous communication, and oftentimes send insult. Yet when that day was instituted there was no thought more beautiful above the Saviour's description than was that which led St. Valentine to devote himself to this particular work.

St. Valentine's Day was first observed by that saint of the third century who loved the birds so well. There are a great many improbable stories told concerning him. But that he was actually a real character there seems to be no reason to doubt. That the birds obeyed him may not in any sense be true, though he may have trained them as modern men have done until he could understand them and they him as few people could do. Anyhow his study of the birds that flew from tree to tree, which made their nests in the spring and taught their young to fly later in the season, which sang to each other from bough to bough, and that supported and helped each other through their domestic felicities and domestic trials, made them to him an object of great interest. He said, "God made the birds as a particular expression of his love of the beautiful," and to those who have given attention to such things there is scarcely anything more interesting than to look upon the habits or the customs or the plumage, or hear the song of the birds. You who have not watched them should watch them.

St. Valentine's Day, the 14th day of February, was observed in the first place because it was the especial day when in that Eastern land the birds chose their mates. It was on that day, or very near that day, when in that climate or that region the birds selected their companions for life. The birds have one wife, one husband, and each was selected for life. A bird is never married the second time. I remember in the country a few years ago that one of my neighbors either by accident or design, I think by accident, killed a little house swallow, and the nest of those two swallows was in the corner of his veranda. The other bird, the wife, whose eggs had not yet hatched, sat on the side of the nest, and called, and called. Night and day her voice was heard calling for the loved and lost. Had he abandoned her? Or had he been killed? Where lay his body? O sweet bird! how tender, how touching, how mournful that sweet call. One morning after the calls had ceased they clambered up to the nest to see if she had gone, and there she lay dead upon her unhatched eggs. She had wept herself to death. Those who have studied the life of birds and their matrimonial relationship find in it the most excellent type, the highest form of human marriage.

St. Valentine, by whom that day was first observed, and who tried to teach all the people of Christendom to observe it, made it not only the topic of his observation, but used it as an exhortation for human marriage. In that land of St. Valentine they established a custom (it may have been a

law), that on the 14th day of February young
people were to choose their mates for a year of
acquaintanceship; that is, they were to become, in
a sense, experimentally engaged to be married on
the 14th day of February. Then for a year they
were to improve opportunities for social and intellectual acquaintanceship, and if in a year they found
themselves fitted for each other, or loving each
other in the sincerest and divinest way, they were to
be married a year later, thus requiring of all young
people a year of waiting before they decided to be
married. It was the hope of St. Valentine, as it was
of his contemporaries, that they could make the
whole Church of God on earth observe that custom
for the good of humanity. If it had been observed
we can see that it would have been a great boon for
humanity.

St. Valentine's Day has been so diverted from the
original purpose that men have altogether forgotten
what it did mean; oh, the sadness of it. The sadness
of the 4th of July that becomes a mere time for
sports, or the exhibition of absurdities; Oh, the sadness of the turning away of Decoration Day from
the solemn laying of flowers upon the graves of the
heroic dead to the playing of baseball, dancing, and
to all forms of sports! Oh, the sadness of turning
Thanksgiving Day into anything but a day of thanksgiving, and the turning of the Sabbath into anything

but that which brings to the mind sacred and beautiful associations! It is a sad, sad thing. Among the saddest desecrations of Satan upon the good of mankind has been the change on St. Valentine's Day.

The tendency of mankind to be profane seems to be innate in the human nature. Profanity consists in far more than simply taking the name of God in vain. It consists in an individual heart purpose to make ridicule or scorn of those things that should be regarded as sacred for the sake of human character and human love. It is just as sacrilegious and just as profane to speak disrespectfully of the marriage tie as it is to use the name of God in vain, for it expresses precisely the same character. If one go before the white throne of God to be examined as to what he has been he will find that profanity means something far wider than in the mere location of it to the use of certain words. It means in the way in which a man looks upon all that is divine and sacred.

When this orchestra was playing that magnificent hymn in this last piece to-night, amid all these sacred associations that make a hymn so appropriate, so musical, if you had treated it with disrespect or regarded it with scorn you would have been profane in the same sense in which it is profane to speak of the sacred and lovely name of God with disrespect.

The ordinance or the ceremony of marriage, or rather the spirit of the marriage tie, is one of those divine things that was established of God from the beginning, in which every heart feels all that is sacred welling up into the worship of God. No man ever feels drawn so near to the Almighty, no man's soul is ever filled so full of all that inspires to the godly and angelic as a young man who becomes engaged to be married to one worthy of him, and he worthy of her, and looks forward to the time when they shall have a home. You cannot express the terms of heaven in finer language than in that simple word "home."

This observance of St. Valentine's Day carries with it a great lesson, and I hope you may never see the day again without remembering something of what was said to-night whether you forget the speaker and the place or not.

When marriage began among mankind it began like the birds, with the instinct of the birds. They were to choose each one mate, live together all their lives, love each other, bring up their families together, work together for their offspring until their offspring could fly away and care for themselves, and choose again for themselves. So like the birds were the original instincts God gave to mankind.

But evil has come in in some way. It has come into life with its impressions in ways we cannot

fathom. It has come to be the work of Satan. The
work of evil has been to try to bring reproach, or
to bring disregard or disrespect for the marriage tie,
and the marriage ceremony is losing its power now.
Men care little, they say, for the ceremony. The
ceremony in itself may be hypocritical, may be weak
because it is hypocritical, and yet as the flower expresses the beauty of the designs of God, in the observance of those formal ceremonies with the heart
behind them is found the most important training
for the worship of God and the love of mankind.

Where it was that women ceased to be the equal
of men we cannot see, but the Bible tells us that in
the beginning Eve was made a help equal to man,
a helpmate for man, so that God's evident first intention was that men and women should be completely equal in all their rights, and each should be
the sustainer of the other, so that both together
might make a perfect one. God said, "These twain
shall be one," and being one each in his place or her
place was to do their share to make a complete, beautiful, and divine home. But somewhere back in the
ages the devil came in, and man began to own
woman. A female child born into the world soon
began to be regarded as mere property, to be a slave.
In all the heathen nations of the world even now
such is her position. As far back as we can go in
the history of our own races we find that woman was

the slave of man, that she was property, that she was valued as worth so many cows, so many horses, so many pounds of silver, so many potatoes, or so many boats. Barter and exchange were made for her through all those early ages. When St. Valentine came in he recognized that. He attempted to reform the idea that in the marriage ceremony or in the marriage relationship itself, woman was in any sense the inferior of man. But he did not succeed. The tide against him was too strong. Sacrilege and profanity have come in, and still creep into the Church, and maintain the things that indicate the heathen state of life.

For instance, the wedding ring is but a reminder of that heathen practice of buying a woman, and fastening a chain to her wrist. The ring that was welded upon her wrist has only become the ring that is put upon her finger now, to carry down through the ages, as it should not, the idea that a woman is the slave of man, consequently must wear a ring to be chained to him.

St. Valentine also recognized the other thought preserved in our marriage ceremony of "giving away" a woman. In this age of intellectual equality, when men and women are regarding each other with a reverence that is certainly according to the teachings of God, how foolish it is to ask, "Who gives away this woman?" at the marriage altar. Who gives her away? Who owns her? Whose property is she? Who has given the bushel of potatoes for her. Who has given any property for her and acquired the right to sell her or give her away? St. Valentine was opposed to all those heathen customs. His idea was that like the birds they should mate together and make their bargains themselves. He did not believe that parents should make them. He believed that they should be allowed to come on the 14th day of February and get so acquainted through the coming year that their own hearts should decide whether they ought to be married or not.

He advocated the fact that the churches ever taught that real marriage is an inspiration of the spirit of God. The Catholic church is right in making it a sacrament of the Church, and it is right that everywhere it should be so regarded. No man can say he is married because he may have gone to the mayor, and gone through the civil service. He may have been to the cathedral and gone through the religious service, and he may have gone to the Protestant church and gone through another ceremony—through three ceremonies, and yet not one of those three made them man and wife in the sight of God. The more ceremonies they require the less likely it is they are married. The real marriage, according to St. Valentine, is Christ's marriage— a marriage of the soul, of the inner instinct that comes directly into a young man or woman from God.   If any instinct is given direct from heaven, it is the mating instinct between young men and young women, and it is right that they should get acquainted with each other.   I believe in schools that bring them together, in colleges that bring them into acquaintanceship, and in all of those gatherings where they mingle each with the other with that perfect and modest freedom by which they may become intimately acquainted with each other.

But acquaintanceship is not enough.   Unless there is a gift of God of the spirit in marriage it is no true marriage.   That was Christ's representation of what a marriage was when He spoke of the marriage feast that was a real marriage feast.   He meant a feast where the bride and bridegroom were so brought together by the providence of God, and so inspired by the spirit of divine love that they knew in their own souls that they were intended of God for each other from eternity to eternity.

If the Church took that view of it, as it seems to be Christ's view of the marriage ceremony, how important it is that we as followers of Jesus Christ should teach and by example inspire the thought of the great and awful sacredness of marriage.

In what does real marriage consist?   It consists in the love of two hearts for each other so deep and so sure that each would sacrifice for the other his own life at any time. To be worthy of being married at all requires that love should be so great that they could live separate from each other an entire lifetime if it were for the value or the good of the other so to do. The love that is a real love is a deep abiding affection given of God, and like unto the angels of God. That is real marriage. The ceremony should go with it that the world may recognize it, that they may themselves be treated as living in that relationship. It is a horrid, murderous thing for people to get married, to come into the marriage relationship in any form unless their hearts have so united that they cannot do otherwise. As the apostle said, "I cannot but preach the Gospel," so neither could they do otherwise than to be married. They could not think in real marriage that any other state was possible. You cannot make a business arrangement of a real marriage.

Then the question that comes, to which I can make only a moment's reference to-night, is that of divorce. When is divorce allowed? We are asked that question as teachers, and preachers, and the priests are often asked, "What is the excuse that is right for divorce?" The Saviour says that if two people at the time of their marriage think they love each other as they should, or if one of them does love fully and the other does not, if in after time they find they cannot live together in peace, and they are

so unfitted to each other that life is but a misery,
showing that their marriage was not a real and
divine one, that cause, is fornication. That is what
it means. It is a spiritual thing. If a husband is
at heart untrue to his wife, does not support her, or
care for her, and hates her or abuses her, he is
guilty of the Saviour's interpretation of fornication,
and for that cause divorce should be allowed. While
I would not advocate divorce, while I think it is very
dangerous to suggest it lest people in spasms of
anger should avail themselves of it when love still
continues, and when they afterwards will bitterly
regret it, yet when the Saviour laid down the law
of divorce He laid it down as wise when there was
evidence that the marriage itself was not that spiritual affectionate eternal love of the hearts which
should characterize a true marriage. Where that
becomes apparent, although they have lived together,
the Saviour admitted of a divorce, and the laws of
the land seem to follow in the teaching of the Saviour in the provisions they make therefor.

Divorce is an awfully sad thing because it ad-
vertises to the world a great wrong, for there is
no wrong so terrible, murder itself not more awful,
than the marriage of two people who do not love
each other. The sacrilege of it is as deep as hell,
and the horror of it the angels of God themselves
condemn. But a real marriage is a perfect heaven.

It is heaven on earth. A real marriage in which all are equal, where the woman and the man in every respect are the equal of each other, and where there is no thought of compulsion, no question of law, no thought of it in the house where each serves the other with sacred and pure devotion, and never thinks of any obligations, customs, or laws because their two souls are so one that each is ever desirous to do for the other,—that is a heaven on earth. That is real marriage. No divorce can ever come in there.

I advise St. Valentine's provision that young people wait. Take, not too long, but a year of waiting, as that is long enough, and in that time keep their good sense, and their worship of God, and ask for direction of the divine spirit, and decide not until the year has passed. When the year has passed if love be so strong that it is irresistible, if there be no impediment in the way which would do more harm than good, if there be no restriction either of human or divine law that would make the marriage a harm to the community or to the cause of God, then it is their duty before God to become united at the marriage altar, and set up their home. "Increase and multiply" was the first commandment of God to man, and it is the strongest instinct that is left with mankind. It is the greatest source of joy to be found on earth.

How thankful I am for the returning tide of good sense in the newspapers, in the books, and in the speech of people. For we have lately passed through a horrid state of accusation against men and women, as though this world was hastening into licentiousness and low, degraded debauchery. I hope many of you have seen through it all that women were more true than all these stories made them appear, and that men were more true than we had represented them to be. When you think that only one out of five hundred men and women in the cities, with all their temptations, ever visit or ever go into association with vile places, oh then the world is better than you think. Yes, it is more hopeful than you think. Think of the homes throughout the world; think of the millions happily married throughout the world; think of the children that love their parents and the parents their children; and while your hearts go out in sympathy for the poor weak-minded who have fallen into those degraded conditions, and you should help them, yet your heart should swell with praise to God for the establishment of the marriage relationship, for the establishing of the homes of earth. Your effort should be to increase their number, and increase the reverence of mankind for them, so that marriage here on earth may be a tie that shall last on forever into the future eternities.

BENEDICTION

O Lord, bring soon about that day when women
shall no longer be sold in marriage, when men shall
no longer be sold in marriage, when that great relationship shall not be assumed for money, or for
title, or because of influences extraneous to the heart.
Hasten the time when Christ shall be so taught that
all over the earth hearts shall be brought to choose,
and when each shall find its own divine mate, and
earth shall be a heaven, an open door, a vestibule to
an eternal home of love on high.

Hear our prayer, and grant us that benediction.
We ask it in Christ's name.   Amen.

III

Abraham Lincoln

(ECCLESIASTES VII:28, 29)

IN the two last verses of the 7th chapter of Ecclesiastes is the wise observation in which the preacher says:

"That which my soul seeketh I find not; one man among a thousand have I found, but a woman among all those have I found not.

"Lo, this only have I found, that God hath made man upright; but they have sought out many inventions."

The whole nation, during the last week, has been celebrating the birth of Abraham Lincoln, and it furnishes an excellent opportunity for one to point a moral or to apply a lesson of the Gospel. It is a very interesting thing, and a very profitable thing to read what the great editors and the great authors of the country write concerning that singular character, Abraham Lincoln. But it is very confusing to see how they differ in their estimate of the man, or the reasons they give for the place he holds in the esteem of the American people.

It is an interesting thing to find that such a character, one who never joined the Church, who never made what people sometimes call an open profession of religion, should now be a hero of the Church, and his principles accepted as principles of genuine Christianity.

It appears to me that the one man in a thousand for whom the preacher was looking is found in Abraham Lincoln but not because he differs from other men. It would be very useless for me to turn your attention again to this great man if it were not for the fact that the lesson can be very helpful.

When a man attempts by poetry or oratory, or song, to put a man like him far up high on a pedestal, as though no man could ever approach him, they do a great deal of harm instead of good, and are disheartening those who might follow his footsteps if they were encouraged to do so. I am not one of those who believe that Abraham Lincoln was so far above all the other men or was so different from other men that he could not be imitated now. I believe he can be followed.

I lived in a day of great excitement in the Civil War, when every side of Abraham Lincoln's character was brought under the microscope of public opinion, and I heard what was said against him, and I heard what people who underestimated him said, and I have lived these fifty years now, and we are finding that the confused mind is becoming more and more clarified with each succeeding year. His influence grows, and his words are stronger now than they were when he died. His great speech at Gettysburg has become now the example of the highest form of oratory, and yet at the time it was delivered it received little applause.

Why is it that his liberation of the slaves, which has become an inspiration to lovers of liberty the world over, at the time it was done, was regarded merely as a military necessity? I have asked this question of myself, thinking that you, with this Spiritual advice, might take a clear view which one should take of such a character, not for the purpose of entertainment or for discussion, but to point a Gospel lesson pure and simple.

Abraham Lincoln did not differ so much from thousands of other men. There are certain circumstances in his life which made him an excellent example of that in which he did differ from common men, and if I were to say to the young men who hear me speak or who may read my words that Abraham Lincoln was a strange, peculiar, God-given genius, and that when his image was cast, "the mould was broken," and that there never could be or never was another like Abraham Lincoln, I am simply saying to the young men, "It is of no use for you to try." But if, on the other hand, we take that reasonable view of the life of Abraham Lincoln that he was like other men, but especially used by the Providence of God, and that there are many things in his life worthy of imitation, we have furnished an incentive to the rising generation. This ought always to be done. There is only one character that was ever on earth, that should be held up above the ambitions of young men and women.

This text that I read confuses people. But it is a statement which I may put in other words—that God made a perfect man, and that since that day there has not been found a woman who has reached that standard in her attempt to make herself over into the image; and that since that day there has been found only one man in all the thousands, and there has not one single woman been found by the writer who has been able to imitate that uprightness which God created in man in the first place. It seems to say that men have a right, by their manner of independence, to make themselves over into something else which they desire to be. Like that preacher, I have never found a man that could build up the ideal figure and imitate the perfect uprightness of the Second Adam. They have all failed, so far as I can see.

Abraham Lincoln felt that he was not a perfect man. Why should we think so, when an age is passed and his enemies are silent, and his friends have become more enthusiastic about him; when we have not reached that state as a nation where we can extol him and worship him as the Chinese do their ancestors? The lesson that comes down to us through the years is that he was the nearest to that ideal manhood, perhaps, in his closing years, of any known American. There may have been a more perfect character of whom we did not hear, but Abraham Lincoln is an encouragement to every young man in this—that nearly every young man to-day has more advantageous circumstances in life than Abraham Lincoln ever had.

Abraham Lincoln inherited nothing above the trials of life from his parents, in body, mind and spirit. Abraham Lincoln's race was that poor white race of Kentucky which has been found there in the years since. You may have read, or may have seen, if you have traveled in the South, those "poor whites," lazy people, that lie around the grocery stores and who drink, who chew tobacco and swear and shoot each other occasionally when they have their family feuds. These poor white people of Kentucky remain, in a measure, something the same as they were in the days of Abraham Lincoln. But those men of the mountains, with valleys deep, with precipices steep, often made characters of a certain rugged, noble kind. Abraham Lincoln inherited nothing from his father and mother for which we need claim praise. Less from his father than from his mother. It reminds me of Henry Ward Beecher saying of his church composed of eighteen members, that seventeen of them were women and the other was nothing. Abraham Lincoln was something. But his father was nothing. Abraham Lincoln inherited no money; he did not come into the world in possession of any funds with which to start himself in life, or with which he could secure an education. I want to say to the young men who hear me, or who read what I am saying, that you have many advantages which Abraham Lincoln did not possess. Abraham Lincoln had no culture; he had no opportunity to go to the schools up to the time he was 19 years of age. As a boy he could not read or write, or scarcely scrawl his name. He had been brought up to hew wood and do odd jobs of various kinds, and lay around the grocery stores up to that time. He had consequently no helps such as men now have to make himself a great man. He therefore lacked that culture and lacked that education; and he had many special misfortunes to hold him back which you do not have.

He lived with his stepmother. His good mother, whom he remembered as a child, died early in life, and the poor boy was left to wander about, and oftentimes he had to live on crusts of bread, and his lazy, useless old father married again, and he

had a stepmother. His stepmother was always un-
usually kind, and was indeed a help to him. But
neither was she a cultivated person. While she knew
more than his own mother, as far as reading, writ-
ing and books were concerned, yet she was of that
dull intellectual grade of Kentucky poor whites.
There are no young men in all my acquaintances
that have the disadvantages that he had. I don't
believe in this Temple to-night any one can think
of a boy 20 years of age that has the disadvantages
which characterized Abraham Lincoln. So I say,
it is encouraging to boys to find out that one, worse
off than they, and having a father of less account
than theirs, has risen to this high station and is receiving the encomiums of the world.

He was chastened in his youth—chastened by sorrow—sorrow of the deepest kind. Loss of his
mother I have already mentioned and you have
read his history and I need not detail it. It was
sad. It left that grief over his childhood that went
on down through the years. But perhaps the greatest chastening was that he was broken-hearted over
the love of a woman. He was of that decisive
character, a man who could love with a great heart,
but I do not believe that he loved more than other
men have loved; I do not believe that his admiration
for her whom he intended to marry was more sincere than other men; I do not believe that he would

have sacrificed more than you would sacrifice for the one you love. But to that life there came a chill, and he, instead of leading her to the altar, followed her, broken-hearted to the grave, and that first great stroke of sorrow chastened that boy; broke him down, reduced him to a state of grief and carelessness of life that seemed never to have left him entirely. He never came out of it even in the dignity of the work he had to do.

He lived in poverty all those years—indeed, he lived in poverty until he went to Congress, and even then he gave away so much of his small salary that he was oftentimes reduced to debt. He was always poor.

He was chastened by defeat; by some very bitter defeats—not only defeats concerning marriage in his first and deepest love—not only there, but he was defeated again and again in his attempt to do something for himself. He tried to carry on a store, and he was very soon so in debt that he was obliged to go out and split rails to pay up. When he closed up his store, he was elected captain of a military company in the Black Hawk war, and before he saw any service the company was ordered to disband, and he enlisted as a private soldier. It is not often that we find a man is "promoted" from captain to private. But it was the history of Abraham Lincoln, and young men may have had like experiences in other directions, and it may have done them good.

Then he determined to study law. As a lawyer he had no wide education, no wide reading. I do not see how any person would ever engage Abraham Lincoln as a lawyer when he first opened his office in Springfield, Illinois. His office was in a very poor building, the windows were broken, some of the portions of the doors were split, and they said his office was never kept very neat, for not many came to it, and he was obliged to sleep in it himself.

To-day we ask the young men of our country to look at this character, which now stands before our country, whose monuments rise in almost every public square and park, and whose life and actions have filled libraries. Look at him, young men! Look! Your chance is far better than his! You have far greater talents than he had. You live in a time when the doors of progress are open, and you live in an hour when men can rise, and rise rapidly to attention and success.

What was it that made Abraham Lincoln great? He was great; his influence was great. We must all admit that. But what was it that made him great—without special intelligence, or money, without education, culture or friends! What was it that led him to become the central figure in our history, where he did certain deeds that impressed the ages? It is reasonable for us to discuss, in view of the Scriptural illustration, what it was that made him one great man.

Many a disciple of Christ has tried to find in Abraham Lincoln a proof of the truth of his own creed, and maybe prove the tenets of his own church. But nevertheless, the great fact remains, that Abraham Lincoln, while he was in the habit of attending church, and while he read the Bible, and while he read religious books, and while he gave religious advice, never allied himself in any close way with any one denomination of Christians. He kept himself aloof for the time. It does not seem to have been because of any choice on his part. It seems to have been a kind of modest under-estimation of himself, or a sense of his weakness, or lack of culture or money, that kept him from uniting with any Chritian church. Yet as a Christian he was one of God's ideal men. He was nearer to it than any American ever known. He was an unright man; uprightness was the peculiar characteristic of Abraham Lincoln.

Now, a man may praise other men who have great gifts—men who have wrought with wonderful imagination in poetry; we may praise great scientific men, great inventors—men who have read the stars, the great statesmen who steer the government through perilous waters, we may praise those men because of some one individual invention or achievement, all of them prominent, and all of them deserving a great place. But in Abraham Lincoln there was that ideal aggregation of all the best traits of human character, making him one, great, round and noble figure, to which the world could look and give its praise; because it lacked the inventions that make up the character of many men.

A man may be a great inventor in words, or a great inventor in machinery, and because of that invention receive great praise. Why is it that Mr. Edison is not holding the same position in the estimation of the world that Abraham Lincoln held? It is not because Edsion has less opportunities than Abraham Lincoln had, many helpful inventions and opportunities have aided him; but Abraham Lincoln had no inventions to aid him. Some may write books. There may be Whittiers and Longfellows, and they may write books that attract the attention of men and women, and the admiration and love of the world, but that invention might be an outside invention, something outside of themselves which they have done. But in the life of Abraham Lincoln there does not seem to be any one special thing which brought him to the place he occupies. He issued the Emancipation Proclamation and gave freedom to the slaves, and that's about all you emphasize of him. If you study his history and try to find some mighty, gigantic outside thing, or invention, which he did to attract attention to himself you do not find it. He was too modest and lacked money to do it. There are no great issues in his life to which he ever could or did go. He was an ideal man, such as the great writer of Ecclesiastes is trying to suggest to us.

He also tries here to suggest the ideal woman. I wonder what that ideal of his was? It does not seem to appear on the surface, although there are many places where he speaks of woman's noble characteristics. The last Chapter of Ecclesiastes presents a most wonderful picture of a certain woman of a certain race, in a certain place, with certain traits, and that is a wonderful ideal.

The ideal man, as God made him is upright, and the word uprightness, when we get back to the Hebrew, covers quite an extensive vocabulary. "Uprightness" means a man of a good heart. O, that's the foundation of human greatness, a great, loving, good heart. And that made Abraham Lincoln a great man, with the help of prayer to God. Abraham Lincoln was a man of prayer. Whether he went to church or not; or read often the Bible or not; whether he believed in this creed, or that or the other, one thing is sure that continually, like Washington, he was a man of prayer. He believed in prayer and felt that his prayers would be answered as well as other people's who went to church more

than he did. He was a "good-hearted" man. O
that means so much!

Milton could write the most wonderful poetry that
was ever penned by man. But he had a weak character. Nelson could say, "England expects every
man to do his duty," and that phrase rang all over
the world, and yet he could be a libertine, and when
we look at many of our great men, even our own
Franklin, we see some things that we mention under
our breath. We find in every great man who has
done some great thing or invented some great thing,
some great defect of character. It is said that every
great man has some peculiar weakness, and that is
true very largely. If you find any man prominent
in one way he always has some weakness. But Abraham Lincoln's character was an all-around good
character. You do not find any man to assault his
motives for moral uprightness. You could not expect to find in the time that Abraham Lincoln lived
any man who declared him to be dishonest. He was
"Honest Old Abe," and he was a great man because he had a good heart, and he was strictly honest
and honorable. He was an ideal man, then, in his
heart, and being an ideal, Christian hearted man, believing in the teachings of Jesus and praying unto
God for help in times of distress, he developed that
all-around character, so that you may put up the
moral statute of Abraham Lincoln upon the pedestal

of City Hall and go around it and examine it with
every kind of microscopic instrument, and you will
not find a flaw in that great, living, moral character,
and that is the character that the Bible is ever en-
deavoring to build up. God seems to show His hand
in His determination to build up mankind into this
perfect uprightness, of which the prophets had found
only one in a thousand. It is to make men like
Abraham Lincoln that the Scripture itself is intended. It is for that that we are ever to preach
and teach and insist. He was a thoroughly honest
good man.

He was characterized by one other faculty, and
that was wisdom; the wisdom that is mentioned in
Proverbs; the wisdom that is mentioned by Jesus
Christ; that broad, every-day application of common sense. That is real wisdom. Man may search
into philosophy and go deep into all kinds of experiments; he may discover some; he may invent something and call the attention of men to himself, but
real wisdom is wisdom like that of Abraham Lincoln, that sees every day some good in every man.
He was a man who could recognize good in his
enemies as well as in his friends; who ever exercised
his every-day common sense; who showed us that
we ought to be forgiving to those who despitefully
use us. The ideal man is the man who makes no
unnecessary enemies, and who, if he has enemies,

tries to look upon that man in the same way as he would upon a friend. Abraham Lincoln's life was a special exposition of that disposition of forgiveness and brotherly kindness. The kind position he took with reference to the people of the South was such as to bring down upon him the condemnation of those who supported Wendell Phillips. I knew him personally, and he often privately said bitter things against Abraham Lincoln because Mr. Lincoln spoke kindly of the South, and spoke of the people of the South as friends and never as enemies. In one of his great speeches he said, "They are not our enemies; they are our friends," and because he approached the slavery question with common sense he had both sides and both extremes often opposed to him. He proposed, before the war began, that the government should raise money and buy the slaves and set them free. The North considered that the greatest possible foolishness and oppression, forgetting how many millions might be spent in the war, how many would go to death, and how great would be the depression in all the after years. They did not exercise common sense. But Abraham Lincoln looked out upon the whole field, and regarded the Southern people as mistaken friends, and as friends who were mistaken he proceeded with his whole heart, and with a kindly spirit and determination, to do precisely right, in bringing about the triupmh of the cause of the Union, and when he was assassinated by a foolish fanatic, there was put a martyr's crown upon his life, that called attention to it so distinctly that it impressed its mark upon the ages as nothing else could do. So martyrs are ever honored, almost worshipped. When Abraham Lincoln was murdered, with his good heart, his excellent intentions, his broad common sense, his statesmanship, his death put God's seal upon those characteristics of the man who brought about the return of the South to the Union, through a teaching which has made them a solid glorious and permanent part of this great nation.

Abraham Lincoln was an upright man such as cannot be made by clothing; such as cannot be made by money, but which is made only by building upon the foundation of Christian faith, upon a large and loving heart. That heart had been broken, and having been broken it is fair to assume that God made him suffer, in order that he might be a better instrument for bringing about peace and prosperity to this great nation, and the setting up of a great people whose ideal he should be. Abraham Lincoln's faith and broad common sense showed him that this nation should lead all the nations of the earth in bringing them all up to that standard of Christian fellowship and brotherly love, where each should do unto the other as he would have the other do to him.

These, then, are the great characteristics in the life of Abraham Lincoln, his every-day sound judgment; his great, loving soul; his prayers to God and his faith in the ultimate triumph of right. With malice toward none, but with love for all, Abraham Lincoln set his faith in God, believing that righteousness would prevail, and that at last truth would triumph. That makes a great character. A small character that lives within its own narrow limits, thinks that all is going to the bad; that evil is everywhere extant, that the good are ever crushed and the wicked are ever prosperous, takes a small, uncommonsense view of life. But Abraham Lincoln was a broad character, who, having faith that all things were working together for good in the sight of God, and that somehow evil would be crushed and righteousness would prevail, became the giant man that he was, and his great influence came, not from the fact that he was a great statesman or a great soldier, or a great scientist, or a great scholar, or great in any one invention, but because of that all-pervading, permanent good character and broad common sense, that sublime purpose in life which goes with sincere faith in God.

BENEDICTION

.O Lord! We read that Thy kingdom shall be found on earth with the ·men and women whose hearts are pure, and who love their fellowmen and reverence Thee.   O Lord! we thank Thee for Abraham Lincoln's great life, in that his heart was full of sympathy for the suffering and the needy, full of sweet humanity.   We thank Thee for his broad wisdom, guiding him into channels of usefulness. Lord, raise up thousands more men like Abraham Lincoln.   We ask that benediction, and ask it in Christ's name.   Amen.

IV

George Washington Day

(REVELATION XIV:13)

M Y text this morning is in the 14th chapter of
the book of Revelation:

*"And I heard a voice from heaven saying unto
me, Write, Blessed are the dead which die in the
Lord from henceforth: Yea, saith the spirit, that
they may rest from their labours; and their work
do follow them."*

My thought this morning has not so much to do
with this prophecy of everlasting life, as upon the
words, "I heard a voice from heaven saying, Write."
That has occurred many times in the history of the
world. I read to you this morning that God told
Moses to write, and we have read that God told
the prophets to write, and we have read what He told
the Apostles to write, so the whole Bible is something written at the command of God. Yet, since
the Bible has been finished, there have been times
when men or women have been inspired by some special degree of the Divine Spirit, a genius conveyed
from heaven itself, which commanded them to write;

and among those whom in the history of the world have seemingly been especially commanded from heaven to write was the great Father of His Country, George Washington.

As one studies the life of George Washington and reads what he wrote, he must come to the conclusion that Washington, a human being, within the limitations of human thinking, could never have written what he did write. He must have written beyond his own knowledge; beyond his own imagination; he must have said things that were among the miraculous, or else there is no such thing as "miraculous." On this day, when we bring George Washington to mind,—and the nation never needed it more than it does now,—let us, as American citizens, as lovers of our country, and as lovers of truth, justice and God,—listen to something he said.

I remember visiting General Lee after the close of the Civil War. General Lee was a fine, noble, lovely Christian man, a man of high purposes, and he was one of the great generals of the world. Although I fought on the other side, yet I always reverenced him as the Southern people reverenced Abraham Lincoln. At that time he said something that I had not heard said before. He mentioned the fact that in the Civil War time Washington's address was taken out of the books of the Southern States which were in use in the public schools. The

Southern States might not have seceded from the United States if the people had read Washington's address. While General Lee had nothing to do with it personally, he told me freely that the farewell address was constantly coming up in a Virginian's mind—although they would not allow it to be taught in the schools, that farewell advice was so applicable to that day of secession. In order to emphasize what Washington said which applied to that time, let me for a moment call your attention to his exhortation. Perhaps I speak too much upon the Civil War. An old man lives in his younger days, and consequently I perhaps think more of those things than it may be reasonable to do. But I know you will overlook my weakness if I do recall the things of my youth with greater clearness than the things of the past year.

But, now, listen, Americans, what the Father of your country wrote, I believe by the direction of a divine voice from heaven. Let us see what he advised which ought to have prevented the Civil War altogether. It was Washington's Farewell Address to the people of the United States. He said:

"Interwoven as is the love of liberty with every ligament of your hearts, no recommendation of mine is necessary to fortify or confirm the attachment.

"The unity of government which constitutes you one people is also now dear to you. It is justly so, for it is a main pillar in the edifice of your real independence, the support of your tranquillity at home, your peace abroad; of your safety, of your prosperity; of that very liberty which you so highly prize. But as it is easy to foresee that, from different causes and from different quarters, much pains will be taken, many artifices employed, to weaken in your minds the conviction of the truth; as this is the point in your political fortress against which the batteries of internal and external enemies will be most constantly and actively (though often covertly and insidiously) directed, it is of infinite moment that you should properly estimate the immense value of your national union to your collective and individual happiness; that you should cherish a cordial, habitual, and immovable attachment to it; accustoming yourselves to think and speak of it as of the palladium of your political safety and prosperity; watching for its preservation with jealous anxiety; discountenancing whatever may suggest even a suspicion that it can in any event be abandoned; and indignantly frowning upon the first dawning of every attempt to alienate any portion of our country from the rest, or to enfeeble the sacred ties which now link together the various parts.

"For this you have every inducement of sympathy and interest. Citizens, by birth or choice, of a common country, that country has a right to concentrate your affections. The name of American, which belongs to you in your national capacity, must always exalt the just pride of patriotism more than any appellation derived from local discriminations. With slight shades of difference, you have the same religion, manners, habits and political principles. You have in a common cause fought and triumphed together; the independence and liberty you possess are the work of joint counsels, and joint efforts of common dangers, sufferings and successes.

"But these considerations, however powerfully they address themselves to your sensibility, are greatly outweighed by those which apply more immediately to your interest. Here every portion of our country finds the most commanding motives for carefully guarding and preserving the union of the whole."

Of course, the Southern States could not heed that address of George Washington, and they passed a motion to secede from the Union, which he had so strongly opposed with a wisdom that has come down through the years. If George Washington's address had been heeded by the Southern States, there would have been no Civil War, and Abraham Lincoln's method of purchasing the slaves and thus peacefully settling the great question would have been adopted. We can all see that now, and I have read that simply to emphasize that which seems in-

tended for us now. It is in no partisan spirit that I
read from that great document.

I would not criticise any party, or the President,
or the Government, except to give constructive suggestions to the American people as to what we believe
should be done. We are not partisans and we do
not believe in partisanship. We are a church; we
are an assembly of Christian people, and we desire
to look at every question with the utmost fairness,
with a conservative mind, and judge fairly and carefully after we have heard all sides of it, and then
express ourselves as American citizens, with utmost
freedom. I have often been criticised by the public
press, especially in the West, because they said I
criticised President Wilson. Of course, I was represented in the papers as saying harsh things which
I really did not say. I did criticise in this pulpit
the representatives of the American people going
over to Europe in great state and expense, and ac-
cepting the invitations to the palaces of kings and
queens, which is so inconsistent with American sim-
plicity. We don't believe in kings. Indeed, we
fought them for our independence, and we have held
ourselves aloof from them, and we should hold ourselves aloof from them now with great care. We,
as American people are democratic in habit and
thought. George Washington and Abraham Lincoln
would never have been found in such associations.

But this is only my personal opinion. Our appeal should be made to the people and not to kings and queens. Mr. Wilson's appeal for the United States could have been to the people, and not to kings and queens. Washington said that independent personal citizenship is the chiefest ambition of the United States. When he speaks against party and against partisanship, as Washington does, with such strong emphasis, he stated that the day would come when each American citizen would think for himself, and vote for himself, and should not be swayed by any popular opinion or movement of party or parties,— to be an "ideal republic,"—and I believe we are reaching it. We are getting nearer to it. Washington's Ideal was that every man (and I believe every woman) should be an independent soul responsible directly to God, each obeying his own conscience to the best of his ability, and each having sufficient education to be able to think independently and then vote independently, and let it thus be a "government of the people, by the people and for the people," and not an imperial rule of one man or one set of men.

Now, I want to read of the things that apply to us and that would seem to be so applicable to our present condition. Open your hearts to it. I try to open mine, try to forget all partisanship, all prejudice, and just read it as though it were "a voice from heaven." If George Washington were to

come back to earth to-day, he could not say anything more appropriate, and probably would not
state anything different from what is contained in
this farewell message. He says:

"It is important, likewise, that the habits of thinking in a free country should inspire caution in those
intrusted with its administration, to confine themselves within their respective constitutional shores,
avoiding in the exercise of the powers of one de-
partment to encroach upon another."

That has been the great evil in the past few years.

"The spirit of encroachment tends to consolidate
the powers of all departments in one, and you create,
whatever the form of government, a real despotism."

Could man speak in stronger language if he were
to speak to-day?

"A just estimate of that love of power, and prone-
ness to abuse it, which predominates in the human
heart, is sufficient to satisfy us of the truth of this
position. The necessity of reciprocal checks in the
exercise of political power, by dividing and distrib-
uting it into different depositories, and constituting
each the guardian of the public weal against inva-
sions by others, has been evinced by experiments
ancient and modern; some of them in our country
and under our own eyes. To preserve them must
be as necessary as to institute them. If, in the
opinion of the people, the distribution or the modifi-

cation of the constitutional powers may be in any particular wrong, let it be corrected by an amendment in the way which the Constitution designates. But let there be no change by usurpation; for though this, in one instance, may be the instrument of good, it is the customary weapon by which free governments are destroyed. The precedent must always greatly overbalance in permanent evil any partial or transient benefit which the use can at any time yield.

"Of all the dispositions and habits which lead to political prosperity, religion and morality are indispensable supports. In vain would that man claim the tribute of patriotism, who should labor to subvert those great pillars of human happiness, those firmest props of the duties of men and citizens. The mere politician, equally with the pious man, ought to respect and cherish them. A volume could not trace all their connections with public and private felicity. Let it simply be asked: Where is the security for property, for reputation, for life, if the sense of religious obligation deserts the oaths which are the instruments of investigation in courts of justice? And let us with caution indulge the supposition that morality can be maintained without religion. Whatever may be conceded to the influence of refined education on minds of peculiar structure, reason and experience both forbid us to expect that national morality can prevail in exclusion of religious principle.

"Observe good faith and justice toward all nations; CULTIVATE PEACE AND HARMONY WITH THEM ALL."

I wish that sentence could be written on the walls of Congress to be read every day!

"Observe good faith and justice to all nations, cultivate peace and harmony with them all . . ." not only with France, and England, and Italy,—but with them all,—TOWARD ALL OTHER NATIONS!

"Religion and morality enjoin this conduct; and can it be that good policy does not equally enjoin it! It will be worthy of a free, enlightened, and, at no distant period, a great nation, to give to mankind the magnanimous and too novel example of a people, always guided by an exalted justice and benevolence."

What wonderful language that is, and how it grows upon me as I read it!

"Who can doubt that, in the course of time and things, the fruits of such a plan would richly repay any temporary advantages which might be lost by a steady adherence to it. Can it be that Providence has not connected the permanent felicity of the nation with its virtue. The experiment, at least, is recommended by every sentiment which ennobles human nature. Alas! is it rendered impossible by its vices?

"IN THE EXECUTION OF SUCH A PLAN, NOTHING IS MORE ESSENTIAL THAN THAT PERMANENT, IN-VETERATE ANTIPATHIES AGAINST PARTICULAR NA-TIONS, AND PASSIONATE ATTACHMENTS FOR OTHERS, SHOULD BE EXCLUDED."

If Washington were living to-day, he would call the attention of the American people to the fact that the very foundations of the Commonwealth of our state, as well as that of many other states, have been laid by noble men and women who left the per-secutions of Germany to come to live in this country. We must not let our prejudices against Germany go so far as to entertain a prejudice against every per-son in America with a German name. We must not do that if we love God and reverence Washington. Because the Germans of our state are a most mag-nificent people, and have done great things for it, and in the days of the Revolution, when they came from Germany, they were "the Pilgrim Fathers," and they took flight from Germany because they disliked its government; they disliked its tyranny, and they came here to be free, and they are among the noblest of the races here. I am sure if Washington were here to-day, he would say to us, as he said in his fare-well address,—

"just and amicable feelings toward all should be cultivated—."

Not an alliance with France; not an alliance with England is going to save the world, but honor and justice toward all nations was his idea, and God grant that it may continue to be so.

"A passionate attachment of one nation for another produces a variety of evils. Sympathy for the favorite nation, facilitating the illusion of an imaginary common interest where no real common interest exists, an infusing into one the enmities of the other, betrays the former into a participation in the quarrels and wars of the latter without adequate inducement or justification. It leads, also, to concessions to the favorite nation of privileges denied to others which is apt doubly to injure the nation making the concessions; by necessarily parting with what ought to have been retained, and by exciting jealousy, ill-will, and a disposition to retaliate in the parties from whom equal privileges are withheld. . . .

"AGAINST THE INSIDIOUS WILES OF FOREIGN INFLUENCE (I CONJURE YOU TO BELIEVE ME MY FELLOW-CITIZENS) THE JEALOUSY OF A FREE PEOPLE OUGHT TO BE CONSTANTLY AWAKE, SINCE HISTORY AND EXPERIENCE PROVE THAT FOREIGN INFLUENCE IS ONE OF THE MOST BANEFUL FOES OF REPUBLICAN GOVERNMENT. But that jealousy, to be useful, must be impartial, else it becomes the instrument of the very influence to be avoided, instead of a defense against it. Excessive partiality for one foreign nation, and excessive dislike of another cause those whom they actuate to see danger only on one side, and serve to veil and even second the arts of influence on the other. . . .

"The great rule of conduct for us in regard to foreign nations is in extending our commercial relations, to have with them as little political connection as possible. So far as we have already formed engagements, let them be fulfilled with perfect good faith. Here let us stop.

"EUROPE HAS A SET OF PRIMARY INTERESTS WHICH TO US HAVE NONE, OR A VERY REMOTE RELATION. Hence, she must be engaged in frequent controversies, the causes of which are essentially foreign to our concerns. Hence, therefore, it must be unwise in us to implicate ourselves in the ordinary vicissitudes of her policies, or the ordinary combinations of her friendships or enmities.

"Our detached and distant situation invites and enables us to pursue a different course. If we remain one people under an efficient government, THE PERIOD IS NOT FAR OFF WHEN WE MAY DEFY MATERIAL INJURY FROM EXTERNAL ANNOYANCE: WHEN WE MAY TAKE SUCH AN ATTITUDE AS WILL CAUSE THE NEUTRALITY WE MAY AT ANY TIME RESOLVE

UPON TO BE SCRUPULOUSLY RESPECTED; WHEN BELLIGERENT NATIONS, UNDER THE IMPOSSIBILITY OF MAKING ACQUISITIONS UPON US, WILL NOT LIGHTLY HAZARD THE GIVING US PROVOCATION; WHEN WE MAY CHOOSE PEACE OR WAR, aS OUR INTEREST, GUIDED BY JUSTICE, SHALL COUNSEL."

It would, perhaps, be interesting for me to read further in this wonderful farewell address of George Washington, for I could not by any reading of mine, or by any sermon that I might deliver, do anything like the good that I do by simply recalling to you, the American people, the sayings of the Father of Our Country. Whoever reads his farewell address, and reads it carefully, will see that it was a voice from heaven speaking as a prophet. He looked down through the years and could see precisely what is occurring now,—as Isaiah saw hundreds of years before what would occur when Christ came on earth. The words of George Washington came ringing through the years, no matter to what party we belong. Let us respect the Father of Our Country, and let us study his words with care, and let us live the Christian life, which George Washington urged upon all the people.

What a great thing it is for the American people to have a heritage like that of Washington. If this farewell address of George Washington's were now put into the hands of every scholar in every school of the United States, the nation would be safe. We would be saved from many mistakes; saved from complications which are so dangerous.

Let us earnestly pray that George Washington's view that all nations should be equally respected and honored, and each one independent in its own place, and yet with one common council, may come. The Lord grant that it may come now, and that no mistakes may now be made, so that out of this shall finally come a league of all the nations, and all the nations have a common, central parliament to decide all differences. That seems to be the only way to permanent peace. It was the pathway pointed out by the Father of His Country; it is the pathway pointed out by the Lord Jesus.

BENEDICTION

O Lord! Help every American citizen to be courageous enough, fair enough, strong enough, to look George Washington's picture in the eye and read what he said and meditate carefully upon it. Let Thy benediction come upon this country, and for George Washington's sake, may it pursue its course onward and upward to greater prosperity, in all things that will make for that noble example, for justice, honesty, and peace at home, which will have its influence over the nations of the earth, greater than armies and navies. We ask Thy benediction in Christ's Name. Amen.

V

Palm Sunday's Sacrifice

(JOHN XII:13)

HOW important and beautiful was the thought of the early fathers of the church when they divided the year into religious seasons and when they provided that Christian minds should be turned at Easter time toward the burial and resurrection of Christ! It was a helpful thought, perhaps given of God, which led them to observe the Christmas season, the Easter Sunday, and this Palm Sunday represented by to-day. The Christian world has fallen into mannerisms and ritualistic formalism, so that the too close observance of these days and seasons has created a spirit of neglect and a lack of appreciation of the great truths that underlie them. If we could only strike a middle, safe ground, not the extremes of formalism nor the extremes of neglect, we should probably get the greatest benefit that can be derived from these seasons of the year. Now, we will strive in a measure to reach that point. To-day being Palm Sunday, it is well for us, without formality, to study what the day suggests and to bring back, if we can, some of the simple, plain history with which this day is so intimately connected.

We do not understand the divine side of the Messiahship. I know that it has a much higher meaning, that it has a wider application, than our brains have approached. I know that in the atonement by the Son of God, reconciling God to man, and man to God, is a mystery greater than can be explained by any human mind. We do not expect to fathom it. He is only presumptuous who attempts to explain it. No man can so fully understand God. His thoughts are above our thoughts as the heavens are above the earth, and he is only insane, or a very foolish, or a very wicked man, who endeavors to place himself alongside of God and explain all that God knows. We cannot understand all the divine relations between Christ and God. But it was intended that we should understand the human side that lies between us and Christ. And the narrative, told in the plainest and simplest language by the apostle, brings forward the chief thought in connection with this day, and shows us clearly how Christ sacrificed for us. This side of His life is not meditated upon enough. Christ made a great sacrifice for us from the human side in this, that he decided weeks before His crucifixion that He would deliberately go to martyrdom for the good of mankind. When He came to that decision He was at Capernaum, at the north end of the Sea of Galilee, His own home. Think for a moment, then, what this Palm Sunday ought to suggest. He started from Capernaum, set his face steadfastly towards Jerusalem in order, as He told His disciples, that He might be lifted up and draw all men to Him. The Palm Sunday which we to-day, in a sense, are celebrating, represents His triumphal entry into Jerusalem, which shows the culminating point of His sacrifice on the human side for us. The cross, of course, is ever in our minds; but this was the crowning point in His self-denial.

Now, when He deliberately decided to die, He was in perfect health. It does not require much loss for a person racked with pain hour after hour, confined to the house, having lost all acquaintanceship with the world, and with all friends, to make up his mind to die. God seems to have adjusted His providence for the good of His people, and seems to have decided that He would gradually lessen the hold upon the world of those who love Him. So we find, in thousands of cases —indeed, in a great majority of cases—that God sends pain, illness, different forms of sorrow; and gradually accustoms His children to the thought that this world is more and more painful, less and less attractive. He keeps clipping off here and there the hold which we have upon the world until at last in the perfection of a saintly life a man is ready to go. No attraction in this world for him. All is in the beyond. A man who has reached his three-score and ten is then living on borrowed time, and is looking towards the coming, towards the future. God is so kind. Now, if He were to take us all in the fullness of health, in the prime vigor of our completest manhood, and decree that we should die, it would be like the awful decree of death to a man who was going to the gallows. He knows he will die next Friday at 11:30 o'clock. He is in the possession of all his faculties, all his strength and health. This world is still so dear to him. Oh, what a fearful experience that is! But if a man chose thus to die because of his love for others and does it unhesitatingly, walks straight on to that moment of his death of which he has been fully informed, it is a great sacrifice from a human side. It is the highest form of human giving of himself for others. Now, Christ was thirty-three years of age. He was at that year in the history of manhood's life when He was completest in all His faculties, in all His possessions. We begin and live thirty-three years up to the highest possible achievement in natural forces. Then from thirty-three we begin to run down, and thirty-three years from that time we have reached the boundary where old age settles in, and a man is supposed to retire, or often to be useless. Now, He was right in the center, at the zenith of all His ambitions, of all His physical forces, of all His brain comprehension. He was at the highest point and yet decided to die, to leave all that this earth had of joy for Him, and face the cross, all for the world's sake.

So then we see Him at Capernaum, starting forth for His last journey. That He knew it was His last is shown by His saying so distinctly to His disciples on several occasions on His journey towards Jerusalem. He explained to them decidedly that He must be crucified, and that He would arise the third day.

Now, the second thought concerning this sacrifice is that He left His home that morning of His journey down the Jordan River, knowing that so far as human life was concerned, He was never to see it again. When He should see it again He would be only in His glorified body. Hence, humanly speaking, He was bidding farewell, as you and I bid farewell, to His old home, Dear old Capernaum! How He loved the shores of that beautiful blue sea; how happily He had heard all the years the ripple of its white waves up its shelly banks, and how many times He had waded in on its shores as a boy, and how many times fished on it in calm and in storm, by night and by day! How many a boat

He had helped to build which had floated out with
song upon the sea! Going from home for the last
time! He turns the point at Magdala, as He is
about to take His pathway into the mountains, and
He turns back to look upon Capernaum for the last
time in the flesh. Back on Capernaum! I know
not why it is, but men who have been born and
lived in the mountains love their home so much
more deeply and cling to its associations with so
much greater tenacity than those who are born on
the level of the prairies or the plains. They that
have lived in the Himalayas of India are so tenacious
of home that they sicken and die when confined to
the plains, though in palaces they live. Those in
the Alps you cannot persuade to leave those white
peaks, those deep valleys, those rushing water falls.
You cannot persuade them to leave the echoing of
the hills because the heart, the soul, every fibre of
being seems to be woven in with the rough cedars
or more rough rock, with the cold snows of the
mountain tops. In the mountains of Galilee, down
in its valleys, or on the shore of the most lovely
lake of all the world, dwelt this man for thirty-three
years. We suppose that He left Nazareth when
Joseph was dead, and with His widowed mother
moved from Nazareth to Capernaum, and from
thenceforth that was His home. He turns, I say
at the vale of Arbela. He looked back at the village

running up the hillside there, and it was just the time of year when it was the most beautiful sight on which the eye ever rested. I have been in Palestine three times at that season of the year, and the last time, three years ago, we rode our horses and mules through whole acres and acres of lilies, roses, daisies, buttercups and other blossoms. As far as you could see for miles, on mountain and hills and valley and plain, it was one great carpet of the most wonderful colors that God ever put into vegetation. As we rode down to the Sea of Galilee, our horses' bellies deep in all those beautiful colors God only can paint, covering miles and miles of territory, it was a sight one can never forget. Why, there is not a flower that grows in the tropical island of Cuba, but what is there. There is not a flower that grows in the frigid edges of the mer-de-glace of the Alps but what is there. There is not a tree or shrub from all the heights of the frigid down to the torrid, or from the heat to the cold, or the east to the west, but what can flourish there. The Sea of Galilee is 640 feet below the level of the Mediterranean Sea, and at its shores you have all the tropical vegetation. You can stand and look up, and within the sight of your eye is vegetation of the frigid zone. It is as cold as the tops of the Himalayas themselves. There is the white peak of Mount Hermon looking over that landscape, being a bright lighthouse for all of Syria and Palestine. Its snows never disappear. Its great seas of ice are ever crumbling and crushing towards the plain.

As I stood, one day in 1869, for the first time at Magdala, the home of Mary Magdalene, and looked across to Capernaum and up the slope of that mountain side, with all its verdure of multiplied beauties, I thought of Christ going away from that home with His face set towards Jerusalem. It was the most beautiful time of the year. It was when the Sea of Galilee is calm and blue and peaceful. It was when the mountains were at their best; it was when the sky was clear; it was when the atmosphere was cool at evening, and never over hot at noonday. It was when vegetation was starting, fields of grain rising on every hand, and beginning to bow their heads towards ripeness. In the brightest and most hopeful season He turned His face from His home, looking back on it for the last time. It is true that His mother was with Him; it is true that Mary Magdalene and others were with Him; it is true that Peter and John and Nathaniel were there; but they could not understand His feeling. He was bidding His home good-by for the last time in His human existence. That sacrifice was for us.

Then, there is another thought, that He was leaving all the friends of His youth. When we get to be old, we make few new friends, a very few of the sincere, dear ones are made when a man has passed his sixty-five years. He does not make new friends; he clings to the old, and when they drop away he has no support left. But here was Jesus, in the prime of life, when friendships are dearest, when they are altogether the sweetest. He was turning away from them. There was the beautiful marble synagogue, built by the centurion, in sight from any portion of the Sea of Galilee. There were the palaces on the right and left, and the wharves and fishing boats, and sails in front; there the rising sea, with sheening vegetation at the rear. He looked back upon that home, filled with so many friendships, so many people He had loved. All His playmates of His youth were there. "Farewell, farewell, Capernaum! Farewell, all My schoolmates! Farewell, all the old beloved worshipers in the synagogue! Farewell, all for whom I labored as a carpenter! Farewell, all who have done Me a kindness! Farewell, all to whom I have tried to be kind! Farewell, a final farewell, all who loved Me on earth!"

Was not that a sacrifice that should touch the heart of any of us?

Then, looking ahead at His journey, He must needs go through Samaria. Then He crosses the Jordan River, is again in Herod's possessions, going down toward the Dead Sea and Jerusalem.

Now, we find Him sending the seventy ahead of Him into whatsoever city He intended to go, showing that He had marked out His exact path. He had told them to go to a certain village near Samaria, then to go to another near Jordan, and another in Perea, and another further down, where John had been baptizing; and another still farther on, and to go ahead of Him to Jericho, go ahead of Him to Bethphage, go ahead of Him to Bethany, go ahead of Him to Jerusalem, and announce that He was coming. There was the most awful sacrifice on the human side of His living. He was going to His death. He knew it would be the death of a criminal —hanged on the cross between thieves, and accounted to be a rebel, murderer, a leader of people to rebellion against Rome. He knew all that. He took all the disgrace of the risk of the publicity in order that in the few days that were left Him He might arrange for the best concerning God's kingdom.

Oh, suppose you knew that you had only three or four days to live; suppose one knew they had only three or four years. Suppose you knew that on a certain day, three or four years from now, you would depart hence; you would set your house in order; you would begin to make your arrangements for your family, for yourself, for your soul. You would look around and say, "What can I do in the

time that is left me now?" Jesus had only these
few days left to Him, and He was going to make
the most possible use of it for the good of other
people. Wholly forgetful of Himself, thinking only
of others, He wondered how much good He could
do on His way. If you will read the story of His
journey of these few days preceding that Palm Sunday, you will find in it some of the most blessed
teachings in the whole book. Calling little children to
Him and putting His hands on them, and praying
for them; calling His disciples and instructing them
what to do after He had gone; calling together a
multitude and warning them to be prepared for the
coming of God; giving those wonderful parables
which have been continuously teaching ever since
that day. So He was using these days before His
crucifixion to the best possible advantage. That was
such a sacrifice for us. I have sometimes thought if
I knew the exact date on which I were to die, I
would like to retire, to get away from the world, to
get into myself again. I would only look out for
my own soul, forgetting that he is only serving God
best and preparing himself best for heaven who is
careful for some one else. The man who is spending
his time on his own soul is mean and contemptible
in the sight of God and the sight of men. If a man
had only three or four days to spare before he died,
instead of preparing only himself for heaven, he

should be preparing some one else for heaven. Then he need not trouble himself about getting to heaven. He who helps men into salvation is the one who is the nearest to God, after all. In one sense, we do need to look after our own souls and examine ourselves; yet, if we had only three or four days left, he is surest of heaven who spends his entire time in prayer, not for himself, but for others. Jesus put Himself in that position of putting His whole time in prayer for others.

Then, there is one sweet thing in His history. I have touched upon it sometimes with all my soul and often have been misunderstood. Why can't we study these things in the light of His human life? Jesus passed down the Jordan River—Perea on the east side of the Jordan—until He came to the ford of the Jordan where He had been baptized, and there He crossed over into Jericho, and there He cured the blind man, and there He looked around among the palaces in which the great had lived, and looked out upon Cleopatra's beautiful garden. He looked out to the cultivated fields of grain; he looked down on the blue Dead Sea, up to the majestic mountains towards Jerusalem, and He was on a journey, the last journey from all these palaces, from all that makes human greatness, towards the little sweet home in the mountains at Bethany. He had been there before and had restored Lazarus to life.

He had been there often before. It was the home
of Mary. It was a home in which He found especial enjoyment, and that human side of Christ's character needs to be emphasized to understand the great
sacrifice He made for us. Thirty-three years old,
around Him every attraction, He enters into this
home; and there are Mary and Martha, whom He
loved, and who loved Him. Young man, if before
the day set for your marriage, you are called to
turn your back on all this joy and peace and face
towards the world as a duty and leave the ideal home
and the wife and the love of womanhood, and for
duty's sake to face a certain death, then could you
imagine something of the sacrifice of Christ at that
time on His way to His death. He knew He was
to die the next Friday, and yet goes cheerfully into
this home, where He had received so much of the
purest, holiest love, and where He had been cared
for with such especial attention. Tell me that Christ
never loved as men loved, and then I must say He
was never tempted as men are tempted, and never
could sacrifice as men must sacrifice. He was
without evil, but He loved Mary Magdalene. I do
not mean in a worldly sense. One cannot deeply
appreciate the holy sacrifice of Christ unless a
glance is taken into that domestic home. They
had set out a dinner for Him. Oh, the unconscious-
ness of it all! Think of your going into the home

with a young woman who loves you with all
the intensity of her pure nature, and who might
cherish a deep hope some day to be the mistress
of your home; think of her welcome while you
know that in five days she will be left alone to a
cold and heartless world. Think of that domestic
scene and the awful sacrifice. I do not mean to say.
that He was engaged to Mary. I do not put any
such extreme inference as that. I mean to say that
He loved Mary and Mary loved Him in the divinest
and noblest spirit. Martha loved Him, and Lazarus
loved Him, and Simon loved Him; but Mary Magdalene called Him "Rabboni." She was the only
one who appears to have addressed Him thus in his
family. We need not discuss here the different views
taken concerning the identity of Mary of Bethany
and Mary Magdalene. Think of their parting, and
He silent about death! Think of her going gleefully
to the door and bidding Him good-by and saying,
"We will meet again," and His reply, "When I have
ascended to my Father." When He had risen from
the dead the affectionate woman caught Him by the
feet, and called Him her Master, and He said,
"Touch me not. I have not yet ascended to my
Father." He must have told her before that in
heaven all things would be complete and true love
would have its fullest fruition and satisfaction there.
Now they part, He with His face toward Jerusalem

and Mary turning back into the house, with a sense of intuitive gloom that comes to woman's heart, which men seldom know. A premonition of things to come which God does not give to men. Was not that a part of His great sacrifice for us?

As He went out that Palm Sunday morning from that home, He started up the Mount of Olives. You know that Bethany is over on the east side of the Mount of Olives. Jerusalem is on the west side, across a deep valley. From Bethany we look down upon Jericho, and the Dead Sea and away to the mountains of Moab. You cannot see Jerusalem from Bethany, although it is only two miles away. Now Jesus starts out from this little village, from the home of Simon, and enters on His journey into Jerusalem for the last time as a free man. He says to His disciples, "Go up there and you will find the foal of an ass there, and bring the animal to me." They bring it to Him; He mounts upon it, and, coming around the spur of the mountain, suddenly the whole panorama of Jerusalem presents itself to His view. I shall not forget the first time I looked upon it; it filled my soul with such astonishment and such a sense of sublimity that the tears just fell on my face. I could not keep them back. On that day Jesus came, and, as He was riding along, it seems that He came to this spur of the mountain, followed by His disciples. Men, women and many pilgrims,

who at that season had been coming up to Jerusalem
and who had pitched their tents and booths all over
the mountain, received Him with wild acclaim.   But
He wept over the city.   "O Jerusalem, Jerusalem,
thou that killest the prophets and stonest them which
are sent unto thee; how often would I have gathered
thy children together, even as a hen gathereth her
chickens under her wings, and ye would not!   Behold, your house is left unto you desolate."   There
was the Calvary Mount, the place of the skull, in
plain sight beyond the walls.   There, on the next
Friday, He was to be lifted and die an awful death.
He knew it; He saw it.   But He saw Jerusalem and
felt her awful responsibility.   He descends the
Mount of Olives toward the valley of the Kedron.
The people recognize Him as the prophet of Galilee.
When they saw Him riding down this mountain,
coming and going to Jerusalem at that season of the
year, that Paschal season of the year, when the
Jews celebrated it with gatherings from the utter-
most parts of the earth at Jerusalem, they recognized
Him, the prophet of Galilee, and their desire for a
king was so great that they were willing to accept
any person if he would set himself up against the
Romans.   Here was a man of irreproachable character.   He loved mankind, had miraculous power;
He was especially favored of God, and the multitude
cried out, "Here is our King; here is our King.

Jerusalem shall be the capital of a great nation again. The Romans shall be driven out and the old worship shall be restored in the temple, and the Jews shall reign once more. Here is our King; let us place Him on the throne to-day!" With that thought in their minds, the people begin to cry out "Hosanna, Hosanna to the King, that cometh in the name of the Lord, the King given of God. Hosanna in the highest to our King!" Ah, a throne so close to Him. The people were united on Him; all classes ready to accept the King if they could only get one to lead them against the oppressive, taxing Romans. He could be a king—a throne so near, a sceptre at hand, power within His reach, and yet riding, weeping on, knowing that in four days He should lie in the tomb as a disgraced criminal! A throne right here for the taking, yet deliberately choosing the way of the humble and the servant and the name of a criminal, through trial in the court, even to the crucifixion at the place of the skull.

How great was the sacrifice of Christ on that Palm Sunday! He could have had His home again; He could have had extended possessions; He could have held all His friends. He could have had a long life of love; He could have had His peaceful home in Bethany; He could have had human love of the highest and the best; He could have had a throne. Yet, on that Palm Sunday, when all the world acclaimed, He was weeping on toward the cross, because, looking down the ages, He saw that it was better for His Father's kingdom and necessary for the salvation of our souls that He should choose the way of the humble and the path of the malefactor unto a death of pain.

Throw your minds forward through this week into the events which followed that day, to the crucifixion and to the resurrection, which we shall especially celebrate next Sunday!

VI

Easter

(LUKE XXIV:32)

THIS afternoon in the wonderful address of Professor Cobern I was reminded of the walk of the disciples to Emmaus, after the burial of Jesus Christ. When He had revealed Himself to them, they said one to another:

"Did not our hearts burn within us while He talked with us by the way, and while He opened to us the Scriptures?"

I heard a gentleman, as he went out of the church last week, say to another: "What are you going to do for Easter?"

When I heard each ask the other that question I began to ask myself the question: "What is the proper observance of Easter? What is the best and wisest thing for any man to do with an occasion like that?" Then I thought of what the disciples did for Easter, and the great lesson returned to me.

Among the disciples of Jesus were Simon and Cleopas, intimate friends, perhaps dwelling in the same house, perhaps partners together in business.

The scene opens with their leaving Jerusalem after the sorrowful crucifixion, after the burial of the body, and returning to their native village.

If there is anything that is sad, if there is anything that tries the pride of a man, it is to go to his native place after failure, to go among his old neighbors who never thought he would amount to much, to go among his own playmates who thought he was foolishly aristocratic and too ambitious when he went away and left them to make a venture upon something in the city. Then to go back after all their insinuations, and after all their jealousies, to confess that life is a failure! Such was the case with Simon and Cleopas. It is a sad experience even at the best to confess one's failure, even to one's friends.

I remember on the second day of the great fire in Boston seeing two young business men as they met at the corner where their store had stood. I was standing not far from them when they met. One had been away traveling as a salesman, and had gotten home after he had heard of the fire. It continued through two days and a half. He had hoped their store would be saved. They met there at the corner. The smoke still covered the heavens, though the fire was under control, after having burned some twenty acres of the best of Boston. As they met their lips trembled, and the younger

man took hold of the shoulder of the elder man, his
partner, and said: "Bill, is it all gone?" Bill said:
"Yes; it is all gone. You see here all there is left.
The insurance, of course, will be lost for the companies must fail, and so it is all gone." The younger
man said: "How can I go back home and tell them
it is all gone?"

They walked away, and I wondered how they
could go home. I afterwards learned from inquiries
of a neighbor living in their suburban town that
they did go home, and that they told their families
that all had been lost. It was one of those bitter
experiences in life that are rare, but so acute that
they burn their way into the heart of a man.

The condition of those two business men was
very similar in its psychological phase to the condition of Cleopas and Simon when they were going
back home after the crucifixion of Christ. There
is no doubt but what when they first told their village people that they were determined to go out
and follow that new Rabbi from Nazareth, and become teachers, and take up the profession of teaching His gospel to the world, their neighbors all
laughed at them, and their family thought it was a
foolish thing to do. Now they must come home
utterly broken and confess that it is all lost, that He
was not the Rabbi they expected, that He was not
the King they hoped to find, that all their time had

been wasted, and there was no more gospel to be preached.

They had lost Jesus. When a man loses Him after once having had a glimpse of Him, how terrible is the after experience of life. Paul and Peter put it so strongly that after once men have tasted of Jesus, once they have known the way of life; that is, after they have had a near view of it, if then they fall away they become like the swine that returns to the mire. Then they go far down. The wonder is that Cleopas and Simon did not have such a revolting sense of rebellion against God, against man, and everything that was good, as to have swept into the extreme of bitterness, and perhaps, of crime.

Poor men who lose Jesus, that lose their confidence in Christianity, that lose their hope in God. I know of no more barren soul than the man who has been a member of the church, nominally so—half-hearted —who did not get wholly into Christ; who did not surrender his whole life to his Saviour, and consequently stood on the edge all the time, not completely over into the spiritual kingdom of the church of Christ; who found some fault with his neighbor, or discovered something that was wrong or dishonest in some other member of the church, and standing in that critical relation it was his disposition, of course, to criticise everything that everyone else did. When he has finally become convinced that his own experience is not deep enough to warrant him to believe that there is much to religion, then he sees and criticises what all other people are doing who belong to the church. He finally makes up his mind to abandon it, and there is not a worse wreck comes upon the shores, not a more terrible derelict floating in the seas to-night than that abandoned soul that has given itself to reckless drifting to its own fate. Oh, to be over in the kingdom, fully landed in Christ, that there may be no possible return.

Simon and Cleopas seem to have been in the middle ground; that they believed in Christ in a sense, not with all their heart and with all their soul, but thought Him to be a great rabbi, a great teacher, a wise man who would make an excellent king for Jerusalem. But now He was in the tomb. He had been slain as a malefactor, and the disgrace of his death was upon them all, and they would rather die than live.

Oh, to come home without Jesus! Probably every one of us have returned sometime from a funeral, and re-entered the darkened home, and felt, "He is gone for all time." How strange it all is! How, without Christ, without a positive hope in the future, without a certain belief that in eternity awaits a reunion, there is an awful gloom in the soul as it

struggles and struggles to overcome the depression
of the horrors of that time of returning from the
grave.

They were returning home from the grave. They
had lost faith in Christ, and, of course, they had
lost faith in God, and in the goodness of man, and
Jesus was sorry for them. What a precious comfort there is in the thought that after His resurrection, when He was evidently in His resurrection
body, retaining only sufficient appearance of the
earthly body to convince His disciples that He was
the same person, in that body which came through
the doors without opening them, that was trans-
ferred instantly like angels from one point to another, then He appeared unto His disciples as an
angel of God might appear to you or to me.

Jesus was sorry for them, and when they were
walking on their way home, dreading to meet their
friends, and thinking of the disgrace throughout
life of the fiasco in which they had had a part, He
drew nigh to them. Notice that He does not reveal
Himself, as He talks to them, and they have somehow a feeling in their hearts that they did not expect,
a comfort they could not have believed possible, an
interpretation of the Scriptures on which they had
never looked before.

I thought when Professor Cobern was speaking
this afternoon with reference to the archaeology

of the New Testament, of a little incident that occurred when I was in Jerusalem years ago. There was a dear, good old monk who attached himself to me when I was a correspondent of a London paper, and he cared for me with a fidelity, grace, and fatherly spirit that was one of the most lovable things in human experience. He went with me almost everywhere; he was full of every kind of information concerning the history of the land. Often we sat in Gethsemane's garden when the moon came up, and he described the scenes in Gethsemane when Christ suffered there, and when Jesus went to the disciples and found them sleeping. This good old monk one morning said to me: "How would you like to walk to Emmaus?" I said: "I do not know where it is." He replied: "It is pretty well established now where it is. It is only a walk of about eight or nine miles. You are young and strong, and I am used to it. Now let us walk to Emmaus." So in the morning, right after breakfast, the old monk came, bringing an extra staff with him. We trudged off together towards Emmaus. We went down into the somewhat depressed, flat country for a mile or two from the wall of Jerusalem, then we clambered up the hill, quite steep, and when we had come to the top he turned back, and said: "You can now see Calvary and Golgotha," and the crosses must have been in plain sight when those two disciples were going back home. If they turned around and looked, they could have seen the crosses probably remaining there after the bodies had been taken down. He said: "You can see the wall of Jerusalem here for about seven miles." We turned every little while to catch a glimpse of a tower of Jerusalem, or of the Mount of Olives beyond. Throughout the whole journey the old monk was full of reasonable tradition. He said: "Now here is the spot where Jesus is said to have joined them, apparently coming up the valley where another path entered this."

The old monk stopped me and said: "Do you know what the Greek word for 'burn' means in its most classical use, as, 'Their hearts did burn within them?'" I said I did not recall what the Greek word was. He said it was a compound word meaning "a fireplace, a home fire, or a fire in the home." He wrote upon a card afterwards what he thought was the proper translation of it, and I went to my Greek lexicon and I found that it is used in that way. In the classics they used the word here translated as "burn"; it meant a "fireplace feeling," a burning of the heart. The good old monk opened up the Scriptures to me as he said: "The feeling of peace in the hearts of Simon and Cleopas was like unto the feelings of those who sit around their home fire in the midst of their family circle."

What a definition that was of the coming of Christ—a hearthstone feeling. Now then read it: "They said one to another, did not we have a 'fireplace feeling' within our hearts while He talked with us by the way?" Going home to the loved ones, going to the fire where they had sat in youth, where the children had been brought up, where they sat evenings to read, where they cooked their food, and where they brought out their dishes for their meals. The "home feeling" of one who, after a day of toil goes home, where the world is shut out, and only his wife and children are there! He sits down by the fire to read some good book, or to tell some tale to his children, and there in the soft glow of that evening light he feels within his heart that restful, domestic peace, which could only represent the peace of God which passeth all understanding.

It was a wonderful experience to me to go to Emmaus, to find the place where the old monk said their houses stood, and the gateway where the gate was swinging where Jesus stopped and "made as though He would go further."

When I came back to Jerusalem I recalled an experience of not many years before, that which made this illustration so impressive. It is personal, but I cannot think of a better illustration. In Somerville, Mass., I was nominated by the regular party for membership in the legislature. I was just beginning the practice of law, and was ambitious as other young men are ambitious for distinction, for honor, for fame, and for office. Being nominated by the regular party which had always had a very large majority within the memory of men, I felt sure of my election. I went to my old father and mother, and told them I was nominated and was going to be elected to the legislature. No doubt about it at all.

But a committee came to my house one night, which undoubtedly represented an opponent, and asked me how I stood "on the temperance question." I told them I was out and out for the abolition of the saloon. They said: "Well, that will defeat you. You would better change your principles, or say nothing about it, or else the other man will get in." I answered, "I cannot possibly do that. I believe the saloon is a curse. If I must say something about that, all that you can say from me is that I am against every saloon in the city, and wish they were utterly abolished, and that I should use my influence in the legislature to that end if a law came up for that purpose." It cost me so much to say that. It was a fierce struggle.

I went to the polls, and remained at a house that was near by all day. Men came and voted, and I saw my friends coming and going. When the time came to close the polls and count the ballots

I was invited to wait in the office of the town hall for the declaration of the vote. When the vote was counted I found I was defeated by twenty-three votes. I was defeated. Broken so that I felt my sorrow was in darkness, and I went out weeping in spite of my attempts at self-control.

I walked down the dark street alone, for as soon as it was known I had been defeated every friend left me. That is the experience of every politician. There was no one to go home with me after I had been defeated. Before that they had made many a kind speech, gave all sorts of dinners, and voiced all kinds of praise in the press and other places. But just as soon as I was defeated not one followed me when I walked down the long street to the corner, and then down the hillside to my humble wooden house.

I sat down by the little grate fire. My wife was in the kitchen, as she did the housework then, and she came out with my little baby in her arm. She expected, of course, that I was coming in triumph, and thought I had been elected, but when she heard me weeping and saw that I would not take any notice of the child, she knew that I was defeated. She knelt down beside my chair to throw her arms around my neck, and cried on my shoulder, and pushed our little baby into my lap. My tears fell on his face until he cried, and I had to get up and lay him in his crib. I went back to my seat, oh, so broken and defeated, and my wife, with her arms again around me, said: "Russell, it may be the best thing in the world. Think how you have not been home through all this campaign. Last week you were not home until after 11 o'clock a single night, and you were called out even on Sunday. I have scarcely seen you since you were nominated. I think, anyhow, we will be happier here in our little home if you are not elected. Let the other man take the responsibility. It may be a good thing that you were defeated." Well, while I did not believe it, while I hated the advice, yet with those arms around my neck, the firelight burning, and the little child sleeping in the crib over there, I could not help but feel what the old monk had said: "The home-fire feeling," the peace of soul which comes in the presence of the domestic fire.

If a man can go home on Easter day with a clear conscience, having nothing of which to be ashamed, no matter how he has been defeated, and if there he finds some loving heart to give him a tender reception, and to cheerfully hold up his spirits through his defeat, he is after all a blessed man. He has not lost. I have never regretted the experience of that night.

A welcome home was related to me by a Confederate soldier whom I met down in Alabama last week. He said he went home from the war with a wooden leg. On his way home he was hopping along from one place to another, and occasionally some man with a mule would help him on his way. He had no other way of getting home. The surrender at Appomattox had left them all to go South, and so he started to walk home to Alabama. He went up the front entrance to the old plantation house where he had lived before the war, and his family were still there, and one or two of the colored servants had remained. But as he went limping on his wooden leg, and he so worn, so dirty, so ragged, up to the house from which he went forth on a beautiful steed with such triumph, he said: "The horror of going into my own home was worse than the terrors of the battlefield." But he said they saw him coming, and they ran out, his two children and his wife, and they caught him by the arm, pulled him down, kissed him, and hugged him, and went rejoicing into the house. Although he had been defeated, and felt all the woes of a patriot who loved his state and felt that he had been unjustly defeated, yet as he said: "When I sat down by the fire, and they brought me some pone cake and butter, there by the light of my own hearth I rested for a little while after four years of service in the army, and there came a peace to me after all, in which I said: 'Is it not all lost.' I have my family, and I can go on yet." He had his house, as many did not, and a little portion of a farm left to him free. To go into that home and be welcomed by those who sympathized with him, and to feel that they believed in him although all the rest of the world did not, was, after all, a compensation more than to be president of the United States, and better than to be a king.

Oh, the joy of that heart that goes into its own citadel, into its own palace—that humble little home of two or three rooms, and sits down by the fire, believed in by those who sit by him, and who love him! They have no word of criticism for him. They have only encouragement. Their eyes are so filled with love they cannot see anything else but truth, hope, and goodness about him. To be lieved in, and to sit by one's domestic circle makes up for all the losses that can come to any man.

How did the Pharisees spend Easter? What kind of an Easter was that to those who had murdered the Son of God, who had sold Him for a "mess of pottage," indeed? How did they feel? They had money. Oh, yes, but what is money compared with this firelight heat, this fireside rest, this burning of the heart in the presence of Christ? What was their money to them but a curse!

The thought is precious that Professor Cobern brought out with reference to the equity of God's dealings with men. He never takes from us one thing without giving us something else in its place, if we only had the grace to see it. He never shuts one door to us without opening another, and if we only had the grace to fall in with His will and turn around and look the other way, we would see the open door every time.

A young man studying for the ministry asked my advice only last Sabbath. He said the doors seemed to shut before him. Men have told me whenever I have related my experience, that they had the same, that God always opens another door whenever He shuts one. This young man had hoped to support himself in a certain position, and when he found the door was shut he turned away in an angry mood, and I told him to pray to God and look in other directions, and then the other door would open immediately. God always deals with those who love Him in that way.

Sometimes we have to be given pain to know the best things. I did not mean to speak again of my personal experience. My father was a very severe man, a very decided man. He never showed any emotion, yet he was kind and considerate, and provided for us well. Sometimes I felt: "I wish I had a father like some other father. I wish I had a father who would take me upon his knee. I wish I had a father who would read to me. I wish I had a father who would say a word of encouragement to me when I had done the best I could, and obeyed him and served him. I wish I had some one to say things to me like other fathers said to their boys."

One day I fell from the barn beams upon the floor, and was very severely hurt, though no bones were broken. I was brought in pale and unconscious. Then my busy father awoke. When the thought that he might have lost his child came to him he became the tenderest nurse I ever had. Mother or sister could not compare with father. Father's fingers were so tender, his hand so careful, and he could entertain me so nicely. He sat by my bed, and ate meals with me. He had never done all this before. I had found a father by falling from the beams of the barn. I would fall again to find another friend like that.

When Cleopas and Simon had lost their Christ, as they thought, and were on their way home, it opened up to them an avenue of spiritual relation to spiritual things about which they seemed to understand so little. Remember Christ was in the spirit, not in the body. You cannot call this human magnetism. He was in the spirit, and when He influenced their spirits, when He awakened that ambition in their hearts it was done by spiritual communication. It was done as Christ communicates with you now by the soul. In soul communication nothing, certainly, could be called mental or material.

God's teaching balances everything in some way. If you lose in this place, and you trust in God, you will find it in another. It is all the time being arranged by some mysterious law of God. Be it in our domestic life, in our church life, in our business life, or national life, or in our worship, God is making adjustments all the time to compensate. Cleopas and Simon had the richest compensation for what seemed lost by that presence of Christ, and in the assurance of His everlasting peace. The good old monk said that he thought Cleopas was overpaid for all he had lost. It had been more than made up by that peace of God.

On that Easter day they were the happiest of men. Christ revealed himself, and their hearts burned within them with that domestic rest of conscience and of peace, the best possible way to observe Easter.

Are you going to observe Easter near to Christ? Are you going to stand in such a relation to Him that He will come and influence you spiritually, and bring to you that firelight of domestic peace which cometh only to the heart that is at rest with God? Listen to Him now, to-night, and resolve that you will not pass that Easter day until you are safely in the ark of God. Resolve that you will not pass that sacred time in the history of the year without being openly fully committed to the name of the Lord Jesus Christ. For to you as to His disciples He would say now, as He comes in the Spirit to you just the same way He came to them then: "My peace I give unto you. Not as the world giveth give I unto you. My peace, the peace of God that passeth all understanding, shall be yours."

VII

Mother's Day

(MATTHEW XI:11)

THIS morning we take especial notice of the gift of God in our mothers, and this evening of the gift of God in our fathers. The text I have selected this morning is in the 11th verse of the 11th chapter of Matthew:

"Among them that are born of women there hath not arisen a greater than John the Baptist."

I suppose in association with our parents there is left some memento somewhere in the house, or will be left in future years, of our mothers when living, and it will guide us into a devotional spirit. I will read a poem by Miss Eliza Cook, one of the standards, one of the classics on this subject, entitled "The Old Armchair."

"I love it—I love it, and who shall dare
To chide me for loving that old armchair!
I've treasured it long as a sainted prize—
I've bedewed it with tears, and embalmed it with
    sighs;

'Tis bound by a thousand bands to my heart,
Not a tie will break, not a link will start.
Would you learn the spell? A mother sat there;
And a sacred thing is that old armchair.

"In childhood's hour I linger near
The hallowed seat with listening ear;
And gentle words that mother would give,
To fit me to die, and teach me to live.
She told me shame would never betide,
With truth for my creed, and God for my guide;
She taught me to lisp my earliest prayer,
As I knelt beside that old armchair.

"I sat and watched her many a day,
When her eyes grew dim and her locks were gray,
And I almost worshipped her when she smiled
And turned from her Bible to bless her child.
Years rolled on, but the last one sped—
My idol was shattered—my earth star fled:
I learnt how much the heart can bear,
When I saw her die in that old armchair."

Directly in connection with that I would read an
extract from one of Dr. Talmadge's sermons, and
one that is selected as of his very best. Dr. Talmadge sometimes was inspired into flights of elo-
quence in which he lost himself, and those were his

best moments, and this was one as he speaks of
his own wild youth and his return to his mother:

"I go a little farther on in your house and I find
the mother's chair. It is very apt to be a rocking-
chair. She had so many cares and troubles to
soothe, that it must have rockers. I remember it
well. It was an old chair, and the rockers were almost worn out, for I was the youngest, and the
chair had rocked the whole family. It made a
creaking noise as it moved, but there was music
in the sound. It was just high enough to allow
us children to put our heads into her lap. That
was the bank where we deposited all our hurts and
worries. Oh, what a chair that was. It was different from the father's chair—it was entirely
different. You ask me how? I cannot tell, but we
all felt it was different. Perhaps there was about
this chair more gentleness, more tenderness, more
grief when we had done wrong. When we were
wayward, father scolded, but mother cried. It was
a very wakeful chair. In the sick day of children,
other chairs could not keep awake; that chair always
kept awake—kept easily awake. That chair knew
all the old lullabies, and all those wordless songs
which mothers sing to their sick children—songs in
which all pity and compassion and sympathetic influences are combined. That old chair has stopped
rocking for a good many years. It may be set up

in the loft or the garret, but it holds a queenly power yet. When at midnight you went into that grog-shop to get the intoxicating draught, did you not hear a voice that said, 'My son, why go in there?' and a louder than the boisterous encore of the theater, a voice saying, 'My son, what do you here?' And when you went into the house of sin, a voice saying, 'What would your mother do if she knew you were here?' and you were provoked at yourself, and you charged yourself with superstition and fanaticism, and your head got hot with your own thoughts, and you went to bed, and no sooner had you touched the bed than a voice said, 'What, a prayerless pillow!' Man! what is the matter? This! You are too near your mother's rocking-chair. 'Oh, pshaw!' you say, 'there's nothing in that. I'm five hundred miles off from where I was born—I'm three thousand miles off from the Scotch kirk whose bell was the first music I ever heard.' I cannot help that. You are too near your mother's rocking-chair. 'Oh!' you say, 'there can't be anything in that; that chair has been vacant a great while.' I cannot help that. It is all the mightier for that; it is omnipotent, that vacant mother's chair. It whispers. It speaks. It weeps. It carols. It mourns. It prays. It warns. It thunders. A young man went off and broke his mother's heart, and while he was away from his home his mother died, and the telegraph brought tne

son, and he came into the room where she lay, and
looked upon her face, and cried out: "O mother,
mother, what your life could not do your death shall
effect. This moment I give my heart to God.' And
he kept his promise. Another victory for the vacant
chair. With reference to your mother, the words
of my text were fulfilled: 'Thou shalt be missed
because thy seat will be empty.' "

I will quote again. God said of a true mother:
"Her children rise up and call her blessed."

Cicero said: "The real empire is by the fireside."

Napoleon said: "The great need of France is
mothers."

Mohammed said: "Paradise is at the feet of
mothers."

Henry Clay died saying: "Mother—mother—
mother."

Abraham Lincoln said: "All that I am I owe to
my sainted mother."

Ruskin said: "Every impetus for good I find in
my soul came from my mother."

The text I selected this morning with reference to
John the Baptist makes the very strong statement,
"There was never born of woman one greater than
John the Baptist." A great man was John the Bap-
tist, mighty not only in physique, but in brain, moral
force, and in vigorous courage. You can compare

him with Cicero, or with Napoleon, or Alexander
the Great, and find him greater than they in every
manly attribute. Jesus himself said: "There has
not been born of woman a greater than John the
Baptist," and thus lays the cause of his greatness,
and places the reason for his power that he was
"born of woman."

You have read in your Bible that expression again
and again, Job uses it, and said: "Man, born of
woman" has done this, or done that, or been great,
or been high. Why does he use the expression,
"Man born of woman?" Evidently because notwithstanding the Bible says so little comparatively
in the number of its words concerning woman, it
does everywhere give credit to the mother for every
great man, and for every great movement. People
have tried to criticise the Word of God, by saying
that it was not fair towards the women, that it did
not give them their rightful place, and yet the
Saviour Himself gives John the Baptist's mother the
credit for the greatness of character which distinguished him . By so doing He showed a knowledge
of the laws of nature that are far beyond our present
understanding.

The study of the philosophy of history, which has
become a very deep and well-founded science, shows
that nearly all, or, so far as we can trace, all, the
great geniuses of the world inherited their special

gifts from their mothers. I am speaking now of special men. When the Bible gives the history of great warriors, great kings, great musicians, great composers, and of those great in the ranks of literature, or of mighty statesmen, it always credits the mother with that gift. It is a curious thing to find in the study of this subject that great men are usually their "mother's sons," and great women are their "father's daughters," in an expressive, moral, intellectual sense. There are exceptions to it seemingly. But the exceptions prove the rule. You recall in your own case, perhaps, that your mother was very kind to you when you had done wrong; that your mother would counsel you, and she would sometimes hide your tricks and disobedience from your father. I remember as my mother's boy—I was her youngest—how she encouraged me, how she overlooked my weakness, and how she prayed with me. On the other hand, I remember my father had a switch—two or three—of the very hardest ironwood, and whenever I did wrong and he knew it, that switch was to come down and I was to feel it—hard, fierce justice, combined under all with a tender love. If I hurt myself, did I run to my father? No, it was to my mother I went that she might kiss away the pain. You did the same. We are alike in human nature.

My sister, oh, my sister. Whenever I wanted to

go on a vacation, or get away from work, I did not go to my father and ask. Oh, no, I sought some time when my sister was especially good natured, and went quietly around and would give her an apple, or promise to do "all her errands" if she would use her influence to get my father to let me go to the cattle show, circus, or some other place I desired to visit. The power behind the throne of my father was my sister, and she was my "father's child." Anything she would ask for within reason was granted at once. My father used to tell us boys : "You must remember she is a woman. She is a girl. You must be kind to her, take care of her, give up to her, and let her have everything she wants." The hazy impression upon me is that if mother had not been there to interfere, my sister would have had everything, and we boys would have been turned out so far as I can look back into history. That is not an unusual experience. It is so everywhere.

The world throughout all its ages of history has been just the same. Napoleon was the pet of his mother. Alexander the Great was the darling of his mother. Abraham Lincoln was especially favored of his mother. And so with the great men of our country. I glanced through a biographical dictionary, and find in every case, so far as I looked, and I must have looked at fifty of our great names, they accredited all their inspiration to their mother.

The great men of the world, consequently, are especially the creation of the mother. They inherit the ideas of the mother. They inherit the mind of the mother. They inherit the moral purposes of the mother. Hence, when great men have blessed the world, we must in truth give the most of the credit to the mother.

It requires no reminder, perhaps, from me, to say that the mother in the home holds the great place of power. Cicero was right about it when he said, "The empire is at the fireside," and the men have the physical and mental strength to rule the world, and will physically rule it whether women vote or not. Physical strength must rule the world whether or no, and power is not going to become weakness by the changing of any of our elective systems. But these men who rule the world, these men that have made the laws at which women may rightfully complain, are the men whom woman made. They are the product of the mother, not only by inheritance, but especially the product of the mother by the teaching at her knee.

The boy does not forget his mother's chair. He cannot forget his mother's advice. Though there may be fathers that are like mothers and mothers that are like fathers, yet as a great rule running through the history of mankind, this is true, that the boy is what the mother makes him. If women should by any means, possibly by some miraculous turn, relieve themselves of the responsibility of teaching the young, they would lose far more than they could possibly gain. Is this government vicious today? Is there wickedness and dishonesty in high places? It is due to the mother's teaching, and some woman is responsible for what these men do. If she has tried to escape that responsibility, she has tried to disobey the privileges and commandments of God. There is no place like the home in which to impress those thoughts and to make that moral character which shall guide in after life, and it is in the home that the mother has her especial throne of power.

Again I repeat it, and it ought to be repeated every morning and night, that women are responsible for what the men do, and the men for what the women do. Men have usually, by inheritance, the character of their mother's line. It is a great scientific truth, not a fancy or a superstition. It seems to be some great plan of God to equalize in this world the relation of the sexes, so that men should not have an inheritance all their own. But that from the male side it should cross to the female side, and from the female side to the male side, in order that equality might still reign among the men and women of the world. A perfect equality, whether man or woman, is the final outcome of God's teachings.

It is an interesting thing to study biology and

anthropology, and find God in them, for students always do. They come back at last to God, and the first Great Cause. Those who have done the finest work, from Pasteur and Virchow to the present day, upon biology, have found that that particle of protoplasm which will develop into a dog, a bird, or an elephant, or a man, are of precisely the same chemical substance. Who then shall decide whether this particle of protoplasm shall be a dog, an elephant or a man, and whether male or female? Who decides this? It is the spiritual realm; it is beyond the physical, for in the physical they are identical. But some impression from above brought to bear upon them guides this development.

After our great Civil War, when more than 700,-000 men had been killed, or had been so injured that they died within ten years of the war, who had to do with the guidance of the results of the war? In just thirty-three years—one generation—after that war the equality had been restored, and it had been restored by the birth of twice the number of boys than there were girls, thus supplying the place of the killed on the battlefield by some dispensation of providence that is beyond the possible research of scientific men. The Lord has decided that the generations of men following one after another shall come along of equal number, that one generation shall be mentally feminine and the next shall be masculine.

The Saviour himself said: "There is not a greater *born of woman*"—speaking especially of the mother —"There is not a product of a mother on earth greater than John the Baptist," thus giving credit here, as they gave it throughout the old prophets, to the mother for the great men. The mother holds a place next to God. So long as it is natural for men to honor mankind, it is natural for a real man to respect and admire all that is beautiful, lovely, sweet and righteous about women. It is natural for the reverse to be the case also. Even with an attempt to shut out all that bias of natural feeling, we find that a mother is a home-making being, a nestmaker, who holds the place of supreme influence in the making of the human race now. Consequently, being a homemaker, she is the nation builder. She builds up the civilization of our Christian age. She makes our churches what they are because she moulds, as I have said before, in that home the characters that are afterwards to touch human life. She is "almost divine," in some respects.

A woman is a very contradictory thing. I do not think a man ever understands a woman, and the way the women treat each other leads me to think they don't understand each other. They are, perhaps, more of a mystery to each other than to the men. How can a woman be so good and so bad? How can they represent such great extremes? A woman that falls into sin or wickedness is more vile, degraded, and hell-like than a man ever can be. But when she is in the home in a normal condition as a mother, she seems next to God.

The Bible says the women shall be saved "by child bearing." I cannot understand how a woman can keep away from God who has a little child of her own to love her here. "They shall be saved by child bearing." The Mormons put great emphasis upon that, that a woman by the number of her children shall get her reward in heaven. They over emphasized it, but nevertheless the Bible does give the foundation thought that women shall be saved by child bearing. A mother's love is so like Christ's that we cannot separate them. No knife can draw the line between the love of a mother and the love of Christ. A mother's love is wholly unselfish, and entirely self-giving. She lives next to the Master of us all in this, that she loves, and works, and sacrifices with no hope, or no expectation or care, for a return. Utterly unselfish is the devotion of a mother to a helpless babe. She gives her life, shuts out everything of experience that she enjoyed, and endures suffering of all sorts and kinds, privations of every variety, to take care of that little, sick, helpless child—utterly giving of herself without thought of how great the sacrifice is to that helpless being that cannot make any return to her at present, and a mother's selfishness never runs ahead in that way. A mother's unselfish love is like that of Christ. A mother's constant observance of innocence and weakness is a training into righteousness, into the beauty of holiness, into an appreciation of Christ's great atonement for men, that a man has but few opportunities to experience. Oh, a mother's love we need not emphasize. You know it. I know it. We all understand something of it. To me it is the great exponent, the great expounder of the love of God. A mother's love for a crippled little child is like Christ's love, as near as you or I can ever appreciate or understand.

Why then do we observe this day of days? Because we wish to praise God for the gift of a mother. The men wish to emphasize it because we are especially the product of our mothers. By emphasizing the mother's life and home, and by bringing our attention clearly to a mother's love, we are training ourselves into a habit of mind that will enable us to worship God through our mothers; and beyond her, through the Lord Jesus Christ. If a man loveth not his mother, he cannot love God. The Bible saith: "If he loveth not his brother, how can he love God, whom he hath not seen." If a man love not his mother, he cannot appreciate the love of Christ. The two are impossible separate, and they are probably always together. The mother that loves with a sincere, maternal devotion the child to which she has given birth stands so near the border line of serving Christ and loving God that it is an easy matter for her to step over, and for the sacrifices she makes God gives her a great return. He does give finally a great return. The love of a mother, if we emphasize and appreciate it more and more, will draw us men, as it does all women, nearer to the Lord Jesus Christ, who loved us in our weakness and sinfulness so much that He gave himself unselfishly, wholly for us. Not for himself did He live or die, not for Himself did He suffer on the cross, but, like a mother, gave Himself up altogether, and gave Himself up, among others, for His own mother. When dying in those excruciating pains, He turned attention to His mother and provided for her. A few minutes before He died His last thoughts turned to his mother, and He said to his best friend, John, "Behold thy mother." Take her to thy home and be a son unto her for My sake. So I say, He who loved His own mother, and in His dying hours of the greatest possible pain thought of her and provided for her, cometh to-day and puts before us this thought, that we may to-day, wherever our mothers may be, do by them as a son or daughter ought to do; and if they are gone, we will bring them again to mind, and let them in heaven see that we love them with a love that is everlasting.

VIII

Use of Decoration Day

(LUKE II :14)

TO-NIGHT in connection with Memorial Day
I have selected for my text the 14th verse of
the Second Chapter of Luke—"Glory to God and on
earth peace with good will toward men."

The sermon which I shall try in the few minutes
to preach is a sermon from that great surgeon, Dr.
Earnest Laplace, of Philadelphia. If I say anything
worth while it is due to the Doctor's promptings as
he suggested this text to me on the train this week
—"on earth peace with good will toward men." It
is not a new thought, it is an old one,—and the
old ones are often the best, as old friends are the
best. This is one of the old principles that cannot
be reiterated too often, but especially in our land
now—"Peace with good will toward men."

We are striving to obtain peace and we believe
now that America is so situated that it may bring
about another association of nations that shall re-
store peace to the whole world. When the Lord
does not bring us into a workable relation with one

system of peace he always opens up another way. He has to this nation given another opportunity. We could not make peace with the conditions that we had; but now we are approaching a position where we can secure peace under other conditions. God always gives peace to His sincere servants, even though they be nations, and now peace is coming to us. There are various kinds of peace in this world. We must not accept any kind but the right kind.

There is a peace by force,—a peace in which fear brings about, that quietness which comes from conditions when men fear destruction. They are quiet rather than suffer. That kind of peace is the one the world has been seeking.

France is seeking that peace with Germany that can be accomplished by the absolute military power to so cover Germany with her forces or so surround her with military preparations that Germany shall not dare to disobey. That is the peace France desires to see in Germany. I speak as a friend of France when I make that distinct statement. Germany's military forces may sometime break out into war but she keeps quiet now under fear. They do not pretend to state that they are going to keep the promises they make. They say they make them under duress, and consequently are under no moral obligations to keep them. They make treaties because they are compelled to do so and they keep the peace now for that reason.

This great principle is so universal in its application that on this Memorial Day our duty appears clear. I will illustrate it for a few minutes. There are homes in which the husband and father is a fearful tyrant. He himself thinks he is not. But he is a monarch who is feared, feared by his wife lest she should do something or say something that would be provoking him. She would disturb the home if she did not keep quiet. The children go about the house on tip-toe or nearly so, they do not speak above whispers because that feared tyrant is in the house. That is a home where peace is preserved by force. There are schools in which the teacher is one of those metallic, harsh and hard types so that the children there do keep quiet. One of the quietest schools in the world may be one where children fear a blow, or a sharp word, or some other punishment, and consequently there is peace in the school. The same applies to business houses where the clerks go about doing their duty for fear of criticism or fearing the eye of some one who is going to swear at them; or they fear the loss of their position or reduction of pay. There are churches where the dictation comes from one person.

I see it continually, men fear to make or express any thought of their own, for fear of being considered unorthodox; or fear of offending the man in the pulpit or the priest.

There are nations which are kept at peace by the emperor or the king or some autocracy like that of Russia. Russia is quiet, Russia is at peace and Lenine is the dictator. They fear the assassinations, the murders, the hangings that might follow action. They keep the peace there, it is peace of fear. That is not the peace that Christ came to proclaim. It is the peace with good will toward men; and the time is coming, for it says that this message is to all people, when the earth shall be at peace with "good will" toward men. A permanent kind of peace is that.

The soldier who claims to be a great patriot and loves his country does not like to see a peace under force, he does not wish to see the people crushed under the harsh, hard hand of law. The patriot who loves his country wishes to have quietness on earth, but the quietness must be that which comes with good will, with good intentions, with earnest and sincere friendships among people. The patriotic men of to-day, brought to mind by this Memorial Day have fought for a peace with "good will." They have not sought for a great navy and a great army which shall expend our territories as in the past. They are not seeking wealth in order that we may force some nation to do as we compell them to do. It may be necessary sometimes to maintain peace by force. It is necessary when some people would rebel. It is necessary to have a police force, it is necessary perhaps to have a navy upon the sea for some small purposes. But for all the purposes of future warfare it is a great mistake to build any such armament. Because it is breaking down and hindering the peace for which we are continually praying.

The true patriot is a patriot who loves to see good will toward men. The soldier who went to war with ill will toward men, who may have gone with indignation in his heart at the time, as it would have been but natural, and who may have in his heart determined to kill the enemy, will cease that hatred when the enemy has laid down his arms. Then the great and true soldier is one who determines that there shall be a peace worth while; General Grant made himself, at the end of the Civil War, most unpopular by saying, "let us have peace." But he advocated as did Abraham Lincoln—peace with the Southern people, friendship towards them, trying to forget the things they had done which we thought wrong and overlook them and have one re-united nation of good will,—the good will of the North towards the South, and of the South towards the North.

The soldier who went to the war,—volunteered

to go because it was the great cause of Christ, when I say of Christ I mean "the peace on earth and good will toward men," was a wise patriot. If all the soldiers of the war had been claimed or had been forced into the war or had been men like Bergdoll, what kind of an army would we have had? Why did we want Bergdoll in the American army? I would like to know, where is the good sense of our people? We do not want any Bergdoll in the army, we are not fighting for any such cause as that he could represent. It would be dangerous to the nation to have such traitors in our army. It was a great and foolish mistake of our nation when it "drafted" men for the army. It should have left it open for patriotic enlistment, and the people could have been brought up to that patriotic pitch where in order to bring peace among the nation with good will toward men they would cheerfully die. But by drafting the men it left the soldier under possible inference of cowardice.

We find here and there a soldier arrested for murder, here are five men arrested for robbing a bank and they say that is the kind that were drafted. But the victories we won were won where the great majority of our soldiers sought to bring about peace with good will among all nations and hasten the time when there should be a universal parliament, and when all nations should bow to the parliamentary dictates.

We are now in a position to open up our commerce with Germany, with Austria, with Bulgaria. Were we now to open up our commerce and begin the exchange of commodities, both parties will be making something out of the transactions and fraternal acquaintanceship would compel Germany for a century to come to do that which we want her to do? On the contrary, the further use of force will sometime awaken the great volcanoes, which are gathering force that by and by will bring on another great world war. We are only postponing war by adopting a peace by force now. The time has come to the American people to seek a peace with good will—to try to forget and to overlook as far as possible, and enter into frank fraternal relations with all nations of the earth. We are fighting the same cause now that we fought more than a hundred years ago when the little colonies broke away from England. They did not break away from England because they wished to accomplish anything exclusively selfish, but they represented the great cause of liberty, the freedom of the people and the independence for each conscience before God.

Suppose we should try to permanently force Germany to keep the peace as that is in the minds of the people still! That would only breed war. The

American people are coming to the Christian view, to compel her to keep the peace by peaceful methods. There are sixty million of people there, and we have a hundred million. Suppose that sixty million people were roused up at one time with spiritual fervor, and those sixty million of people were to be united with good will to each other, with friendships, tried and true to themselves and their nation, it would take the whole world again to conquer Germany. Suppose sixty millions of people were all we had in this country, suppose some conqueror were to assail this country when we had sixty million people roused to a patriotic fervor, a determination in the sight of God and in the sight of man to resist unto death. Our own flag and our own nation would stand against the world. For when our colonies rebelled against England, England was a mighty empire on which the sun never set, the greatest in the world, and these poor little colonies over here had an army less than 100,000 to put against an empire. See what they accomplished and fought out because of the absolute common consecration to the cause of human liberty, with the determination to stand together through starvation.

If Germany shall by and by feel so oppressed or so unfairly dealt with; reduced it maybe to less than she has now, yet that people once aroused with that common instinct of self-preservation will believe that their cause is the cause of God. Nowhere on the earth can an intelligent people be conquered if they are united with a common good will towards each other and toward God.

Germany is now divided into her provinces, her political parties quarrel among themselves, hence she is very weak now. But when the coming of that spirit of fraternity shall unite them all in one conscientious union then what are navies, what are armies?

I would not state that we now have any reason to fear Germany. I want to illustrate what might be if we strive to keep peace by force. Force can only end in revolution, and what the revolution will bring forth no man can foresee.

Japan is not fully peaceful with us, and she has reason to feel that way because of discrimination against her citizens when they come into this country. They are not allowed the same privileges in the ownership of property or in becoming citizens, as are other nations. We cannot blame them for feeling they are wronged under oppressing conditions like that. We must move very slowly in our reforms, yet must express our good will to Japan very soon or else there is warfare on the Pacific. With France or England on her side and Russia her ally how great will be the warfare for the years to come, a warfare of force, warfare of ill will.

We must not submit to things that are shameful, to things that are weak, and we are not to show cowardice, but we are to show good will, and treat Japan fairly so that the people of Japan will love us, that the people of Japan may turn in with us and help us. We may need them by and by.

They want peace in Ireland; and they are quite sure to have peace there now; and it is better to have peace of some kind than to have none. There is no question but what old England is aroused now and when England really feels excited there is going to be a large army in Ireland; and when they fill every village and every farm in all of Ireland with soldiers there will be a peace. But do you think it will be a permanent peace? Can it be permanent under such conditions? They may for a while accomplish this purpose, but the one great end will not thus be secured,—the peace of good will.

I was in West Virginia this week and I went over that region in the mining strike, where they have been fighting so fearfully of late, where they have been shooting each other on the street and across the little river and carried it on for months; and they have called out the troops to quell the rebellion. I talked to the people and saw the train that had been fired upon a day or two before. They told me there would be no peace there until there was "good will," until the owners of these mines were willing to meet the miners on an equal basis and treat them like free men. There must sometime be good will. The only thing that can bring peace to the mining strikers in West Virginia is the advocacy of the cause of Jesus Christ,—good will to men— and the nation ought to insist that in West Virgina there shall be good will, or else those people be scattered where they will be too weak to disturb in any united movement. Something must be done to accomplish good will between the strikers and their employers. It is astonishing how a little ill will can bring about great terrific results.

Did it ever occur to you that America still is ruled by so few people? This boasted democracy where men and women have a right to vote, each the equal of any other. How few people rule this empire, how few. We support our courts and pay their expenses, we use police force throughout the city and pay their expenses, we give up our rights to go to certain places and do certain things, surrendering our rights in order that they may capture or keep quiet a few criminals. To that extent the criminals rule. They say there are more murders since the war. But I have sometimes counted up in the newspapers the number of murders and wondered why there were so few in a nation of one hundred million. A hundred million give up their rights because these few criminals occupy such a place of danger; that little minority of criminals are really controlling the vast majority.

We passed the great prohibitory amendment in which a hundred million people give up their right to take certain things which they think harmless, while many of them thought it did them good. Thus a few men command the many. The amendment was passed, and there is more rum sold and more profits made. It requires only an open eye for a day to see that there is more rum sold now than ever before; more people drunken now. They get it now clandestinely and the government gets no tax on it. It has spread far and wide and yet when I read in the paper of the number who were arrested for drunkenness, and out of two million people thirty-eight were arrested for drunkenness, and in two days fifty-eight only of two million were drunk. But because they were drunk, we of the two million surrender our wishes in the matter, all of which we feel it a duty to do. Because there are only a few people who do these things that are wrong, we are governed by a very small minority. There is always a time in the history of a nation when a single individual must be its dictator, when one man must have all power in order to accomplish what the nation should accomplish; we had it so in Wilson's administration, we made him emperor of the country, because it was better that the minority of one out of one hundred million should control the whole country. The small minority that control this country is shown in the peace we have at home. In the city of Philadelphia there are a few men who really control our political affairs and the number is amazingly small. When you wish to accomplish something for the public good you do not have to see more than a few people in Philadelphia to accomplish anything you desire if they agree with you. It is a peace rule; sometimes it is a very dangerous rule, sometimes a good rule. But the American democracy is governed by a very few people. But if these few people have in their hearts "good will" then it is the best government in the world.

There is no government better than a kingdom. Christ is the King of the Christian kingdom. There is no government of better form than the one which has a few people to control the government, provided "good will" be in the heart of the president or the emperor or in the hearts of the autocracy—provided always that their purpose be true. Then they are the fathers of their people and the people can go their peaceful way and trust the administration to them. All nations must have their leaders and to get good will among these leaders is our first great duty. We must get good will in our president, in our Senate, in the courts among the judges, among all parties. We must do this with reference to the administration of law. We must be sure that the people have good intentions.

Now the peace of the future depends very much upon President Harding and we must pray for him, work with him and his great influence should be used to bring about peace upon the earth, friendships, solid good will.

We are now desirous of organizing a new society that shall preserve all that has been done and unite all nations in one common association for the purpose of peace. That is the work of this nation and on this Memorial Day when we are thinking of those who have died for the country. We should pray heartily that the government of our nation may have a good will towards all nations of the earth, that it may entertain no hatred of any nation, entertain no prejudices, may have no disposition to be jealous of any nation but that it may be high and noble in its purposes, honest in its hearts, to be a friend of every nation on the face of this earth. Then shall we have the peace we are talking about now. Then shall we accomplish what the Lord came to accomplish. He said to all people there shall come a time when there shall be peace on earth with good will toward men. Let us drop our animosities, let us drop our hatred, let us get rid of our unfair competition, let us go in as a nation into the coming year with a determination that the principles taught by Jesus Himself shall be wrought out into the association of nations, very soon to come. Now they have a "league of nations" in which Germany is to be shut out. We cannot have any league of nations that shall bring about peace until all nations, without exception, come into it and with good will towards each other shall support its parliament and execute its decrees.

BENEDICTION

Oh Lord grant unto us that we may have peace in our homes, the peace that cometh from loving, good will among all people in that home and we pray Thee that in school, in business, in public affairs, in the Church we may have that peace which cometh from the loving determination to sink one's self in help of his fellowmen; and we pray for the peace among the nations which shall arise from the determination of all people to be fraternal, trustful, forgiving and faithful in all things towards each other, and we pray that this coming of Christ, of peace with good will toward men, may be promoted on the morrow's Decoration Day,—may it have its influence upon our nation and our nation upon the nations of the earth and may we feel that we have been drawn nearer to the peace that shall be permanent, to that peace of God which passeth all understanding. We ask it in Christ's Name. Amen.

IX

Sure to Blunder

(ISAIAH XL:31)

IS this valley above the snake line?" Tlat question sounds queer to any one who does not know the Berkshire Hills of Massachusetts. Have you gloried in the myriad shades of living green, the fascinating, inviting glens and dear, lover-like nooks? Well! well! You have something yet to see. I think there are many gorgeous landscapes yet unseen by the oldest boy. But the Berkshires, so famous among poets, artists and novelists, are so accessible! But I began to speak about the snake line. It is not an imaginary line, although no one could stick a pin into the strange boundary. It is about twelve hundred feet above the level of the sea. All above that line on the mountain tops is a forbidden territory to poisonous snakes. For some strange reason even the professors of natural history do not explain why those wriggly, sneaking, hissing, crawling, assassinating serpents are forbidden to go farther up the hills of God. They can curl in the leaves and watch for a deadly strike, when under beds of colored lilies down on the plain, or they can peak out of their holes in the earth and leap forth at foxes, dogs, horses, cows or men who innocently come near. But they must stay below the line. Boys, girls and preachers can go out safely into thickets, climb cliffs and feel their way through dark forests of pine or cedar, if they only are careful to keep above the snake boundary. But down nearer the sea level, death lurks under the blueberry bushes, and the rattlesnakes bite the barefooted boy seeking blackberries by the highway. A very rich family from Newport placed their cottage in a lovely but low valley near the Hampshire Highlands of the Berkshire range, and one day a girl visitor was so bitten that the poison left her a cripple, and it was a hard task to save her life. Poor thing! Her father had millions, but she visited friends who lived below the snake line. Those who live on the mountain tops are not in such danger because the God of nature says to the fanged assassin, "Keep down in the low lands and hide in the swamps, or die." So when the serpents used to be more plenty and their bites less curable by antidotes, the first inquiry by a new settler was always, "Is the land above the snake line?" If the hill or valley where he wished to place his home was below the snake border it could not be sold to any wise one for a home. Dwellers down there used to get up in the morning and find long creatures coiled under their beds, and children have been found playing with poisonous serpents on the front veranda or on the barn floor. It is not a pleasant thing to think about or to talk about, so we will come at our gospel by another route. You have seen an eagle's nest, perhaps, in a museum or zoölogical garden, or in a picture, and the birds who build them are strong, hardy, wise birds. They always make their majestic homes above the snake line, and they consider it to be their business, too, to make the valleys safer below the strange boundary.

There was a deep valley near an old homestead in the Berkshire, and I knew a boy once who used to watch the eagles while he was going after the cows, evening after evening. The old father eagle would fly down the valley and light on an old broken tree, and watch and watch for his enemy, the poisonous rattler. If he caught a glimpse of the speckled serpent down by the brook or in the tall grass, he would patiently sit there and wait with his great wings half spread, ready for a fatal swoop down on the snake. Sometimes when the watch lasted several days the old gray mother eagle would take the father's place while he went off fishing or foraging elsewhere to support their little family up among the rocks. But one or the other was sure to be on hand when the serpent became careless and risked a bath in the sunshine. The boy reported often week after week that the old eagle was still watching on that crag, and the boy's father would say, "Oh, yes, the old bird is wise enough to know that snakes have too little sense to keep out of sight long." Even the oldest serpent was sure to blunder somewhere some day. The assassin in his hole knew that he was not permitted to enter the paradise of the hill tops, but he judged other people by himself and concluded that an eagle was as uneasy and careless as himself. He miscalculates; he blunders. The greatest victories of history have been most often won through some blunder of the enemy. A great general counts on that, and watches for the mistakes of his enemies. The Devil, all evil men, all liars, all thieves, and all sinners are blunderers. It is always a foolish mistake to do wrong. Sin is snake-like foolishness; and in time his wickedness will ensnare the evil doer himself. In any game or sport, like tennis, baseball, racing or household plays, the mistake of your opponent counts for you. So in the awful contests of good men and angels with the leaders of evil, the sinner will give over the battle by some silly blunder, and will in any case finally fail, if the eagle or a good man or woman watches and waits long enough. So the eagle, like a brave Christian, is not only a resident above the society of the wicked, but he goes down into the infested valley and gives battle to the serpents who lurk for the lives of men.

Sometimes the cowboy would wonder why God made any serpents, and why God let wicked men and temptations to wrong exist in the world anywhere. But he did not find out why. He concluded that he was not to know why, but decided that he did know that there are evil boys and evil girls, and poisonous snakes in the world, and hoped he would never be like them.

At last that old sentinel eagle was rewarded, for his vigil, and the horrid serpent ventured out to seize a beautiful innocent bird which flew down to the brook for a bath. Then like a lightning stroke the vengeance of God in the eagle swooped down with sharp talons and bayonet beak, and when the boy looked far up in the sky the great wings of the eagle slowly swept dignifiedly through the upper air toward the Eyrie where the applauding family waited for the warrior's return, and in the hard talons of the great bird swung along the poisonous reptile, harmless and dead.

Boys, girls, men, all, who are human, have the strange privilege of choosing whether they will be poisonous snakes or majestic eagles. They can choose to live out of evil associations above the snake line. They can help up and defend those who are still down in evil temptations and in dangerous localities. They can watch and wait and in due time in the power of God swoop down upon evil and bear

off in triumph the enemy of Christ. Boys! choose
your home, and in thought, feeling, intention and
companions, live ever above the snake line. Be like
unto the eagles mentioned in the fortieth chapter of
Isaiah, where it says that "they that wait upon the
Lord shall renew their strength and shall mount up
with wings as eagles."

X

"Graduation Thoughts"

(DEUTERONOMY XXX:19, 20)

THIS morning my text I have chosen from the
30th chapter of Deuteronomy, the 19th and
20th verses:

*"I call heaven and earth to record this day against
you, that I have set before you life and death, blessing and cursing: therefore choose life, that both
thou and thy seed may live;*

*"That thou mayest love the Lord thy God, and
that thou mayest obey his voice, and that thou mayest
cleave unto Him: for He is thy life, and the length
of thy days; that thou mayest dwell in the land which
the Lord sware unto thy fathers, to Abraham, to
Isaac and to Jacob, to give them."*

My text is almost wholly included in the expression,

"Therefore choose life!"

In the last sixty years it has been an almost an-
nual occurrence with me to be present at some com-
mencement exercises, and in the last forty years
there has hardly been a year, that I have not been

present at some college, university or school anniversary in connection with the baccalaureate address. Yet, in graduations from university or college, there is not such opportunity to say the most important things that should be said to mankind, as there is at the graduation from the high school.

We welcome these young men and professors today with a feeling of responsibility, a feeling that it is an especially opportune moment. It is a psychological moment in the lives of these young men, in which we may all learn a great Gospel lesson.

Usually at the end of the high-school term, the greatest question before every graduate is, "What shall I do in life?" There is no place in life where young men and women come so immediately face to face with the all-important question, "What shall I do with my talents? What profession shall I take up? What business shall I enter? What occupation will be most prosperous for me? What will bring me the most happiness in life? What will give me the greatest opportunity to make others happy? What will give me the greatest opportunity for the service of the living God? As the life's calling?"

In order to consider the question from the Gospel standpoint, we need to consider our limitations. It is usual for mankind to look only on one side of a question, so that if it has three sides they see only one-third of it. It is usual for a man to say, "I can make my way; for other men are self-made." "Indeed all men are self-made who succeed; I can be a self-made man," looking only at what he can do himself. Others look entirely at their environment and they say, "I am so situated that I cannot be this, that or the other," and many of them decide they cannot be anything or do anything. Then there is another side, which is a man's inheritance. "I am what I have inherited and cannot expect to be anything else." Therefore to these young men this morning, as to all who listen, I come bringing an old man's advice.

The first thing I desire to mention is your limitations. You did not choose your parents, and in many cases you think you could have done better if you had. You did not choose your home or your country, and many of you wish you had had an opportunity to have chosen the country in which you were born. You could not do that. That is a limitation beyond which you could not go. You have inherited from your parents certain traits of character coming down through generation after generation and you are not responsible for that. You had no choice in the matter. Neither God nor man holds you responsible for traits of character you inherited which are beyond your control. Many of you are so situated. You did not choose the world in which to be born. If you had been consulted you might have chosen Mars or Uranus or some distant constellation of the universe; you might have chosen some other world to be born in, and I have seen a great many people who would have chosen some other universe if they had had their choice. But that was beyond them. We cannot hope either to be born on Mars or Alcyone. We would choose, I say, our native country. Think how many foreigners sing "My country, 'tis of thee I sing," and yet they are singing of America; when their own native country is far away. It is an inconsistency they often wish they could have avoided. But it was a condition we could not change. It was fixed, eternal. We cannot hope to change that. Hence it is useless to kick against the pricks and try to overcome that which is altogether beyond our power.

We wish we had inherited different bodies. Our bodies may be weak in many ways. We wish that our parents had so lived, or had been of such a class as to have imparted to us the physical power of endurance. How many young men would like to be soldiers, like these who are here before us this morning in their uniforms to-day. They, too, want to be soldiers, yearning to be warriors, but the government says "Your eyes are weak" or "your heart is weak and you would be more of a hindrance to the government than you would be a help." So many a young man regrets the inheritance of his body.

But he is in the limitations of that body. How often we see men of a remarkable memory, and I often have seen men with such memories and I have said, "I wish I had a memory like that, or that genius for definite things which led them to choose what they should do in life, and who have gifts that you and I have not." The man who is going to succeed in life must not over-estimate himself. He must not think that he can be a carpenter when he is unfitted for that calling; he must not think that he can be a teacher or even a soldier when he is unfitted for it. He must do the thing for which he is naturally fitted, and consequently you must examine yourselves with the greatest care. Find out what you are fitted for. Don't over-estimate yourself, which is the greatest danger, but study yourself, and remember, however unfortunate you may be, you are obliged to live with yourself. You are your own most intimate companion; you are your nearest companion; you are your nearest company; you are your own adviser; you live with your own self, young man! Do you not pity some young men who have to live with themselves? Of all things that attract the sympathy of the sincere mind, that is perhaps the keenest of them all! When you think of their disagreeable, inherited bad traits of character having certain definite weakness of mind, and then remember that they have to live with themselves night and day, never getting away from their own society, and that "every person is known by the company he keeps," you cannot escape a feeling of hearty sympathy. Such a person is certainly the best representative of that old proverb. We must remember that we cannot be some one else. We have a soul; an independent identity, a personal spirit; something inside of the body; something eternal, unchangeable, a human soul! We have that, and it is our own soul. We have not some one else's soul. We have temptations to sin that other people do not have. Other people seem to go through the world without having any trouble; seem to have no great temptations to bear. Yet we cannot change it.

We cannot change our environment. We are born of a certain race and associated with them. We cannot expect to be anything else. A man is born a Jew and he is with the Hebrew people and he has certain tendencies of that racial life; others may have been born in Ireland with Irish associations, another may be born in England or in Italy, and each one is in that environment in spite of himself. It might not have been what one would have chosen. You have been to one of the best schools in the United States, and you have been associated there with kindred spirits of young men of your kind, of your grade of thinking, of your environment, and you need not expect to change that environment.

Consequently, you must take an inventory, if you are going to choose now what you are going to be. This is your day for doing it! This is your day to shape your course so as to avoid weakness; so as to avoid the dangers that specially assail you; this is your day to avail yourself of every possible advantage which your genius or makeup have given you. You have special gifts of mind, every one of you. You may say, "I am not a genius," but you are. No two young men are alike. God never made two men just alike. Every single young man in this graduating class has some one definite gift of mind no one else has, and if he uses that to the best advantage he has an open road. It is the open door for every young man who takes an inventory of his own life. You must take an inventory of what capital you have; of what money you save, although that is of the least importance. You must take account of what family influence you have; you must take account of the number of friends you have. A young man who goes to school or college, surrounds himself with a great many friends or should do so. A person who belongs to a church like this should have at least a thousand personal friends. The church gives him the opportunity of making them, and they are capital beyond valuation. They are worth far more than money, and the more you use them rightly, the happier they will be, and you will be of the more use to them.

You are to take account of God's laws which are in the universe, and be careful that you do not run against those eternal, ongoing laws which you cannot change. God has set down certain great moral and religious laws, which are fixed, eternal, and woe unto the man who throws himself against them. So you must take account of stock, and you must use nature's forces. The great river runs down the valley, and if you put your boat in that river you will be crushed upon the rocks, and you know it, but if you use your engineering powers and build up a great dam and hold back the forces of the river, and turn it into a single stream and put it at work, it does the work of a thousand men, and it serves you faithfully day by day. You can use God's laws; you can use His forces; you can turn them in for yourself and they will be your capital. If we will study our natural tendencies carefully, we will be able to decide what is best to be done.

O! this is an immortal moment for you, young man! You may have come to church as a matter of form; you may have come to church because you were invited; you may have come to church, perhaps, because it is usual to do these things at the end of the graduating term. But you are nevertheless here in the Providence of God. You are here for a definite purpose and you are here to be called upon by your God to decide what you will do for yourself. Because while we cannot change many of our environments, we have a certain liberty; we have a certain line put like a circle around us, in which we have absolute choice, and Joshua said to the men of Israel, "Choose ye this day whom ye will serve." So in every man's life there is the power to choose within certain lines, and within those limits he can so decide as to make life a great success.

The wise way to decide how to be the most successful is to learn what the world needs. What does the world need in business; what does the world need in agriculture; what does the world need in the professions; what does the world need in art, in music, in religion? Decide what is the most needed thing and put your self in the place where you will be most needed. Look around you and see what men like you can best do, and then decide where such a man can best invest his life; so that you may study human nature; so that you may study commerce, so that you may study business, philosophy, in order to find where a man with your peculiar makeup can best invest himself to the greatest profit both for himself and others. For he who seeks the Kingdom of God first, helps his fellowmen the most, and is always doing the most for himself. All those things will be taken care of. Consequently invest yourself where you are most needed. You are called of God, every one of you, no matter to what denomination you may belong, no matter what your family connections, or your life or your race, you are called to God, and you must decide where that call leads you. To be called of God is to be called to the service of one's fellowmen, to be called of God is to be urged to do something that you can do, and to do something you can do best; consequently all our study exhorts us to hear the voice of God so distinctly that we will know for certain. You may feel an inclination toward a profession, and it may be the voice of God calling you, and yet the voice of conscience, the voices of nature and environment and the needs of all mankind must enter into the call, and all those voices must harmonize into one great and grand anthem calling you into the service of your God. ,

Let me say when you make these choices choose religion! It is an old-fashioned term; you have heard it very often; over and over again, but it is new to every one who starts in life, and it is new to you who are here this morning, and remember that however much money you may make in gambling, or in underhand investments, the laws of God are fixed. Sin may be hidden for a while, but somewhere, sometime your sin will find you out, and a departure from the laws of God, from the dictates of your own conscience, will bring you retribution, as sure as the night follows the day. Remember that, and consequently never enter into any unrighteous calling.

One day there was a steamer went out from New York, one of the greatest steamers that ever came across the ocean. I traveled upon it twice, and the luxuries of that steamer were greater than that of any palace. It was filled with passengers, men, women and children, and before it reached the shores of England it was sunk by an assassinating submarine, that German assassinating dagger of the sea! and the ship went down, and the waves were filled with the dying and the drowning, and from this church there went one of the sweetest little families that ever walked the earth. It was a great, great sin. It was a great, great wickedness! It was a national crime, thus to attack the innocent, the undefended, the weak, the women and children and the peaceable citizens. It was a great, national crime! Now, friends, what do you see?

Riding through the country as I do, I see miles and miles of wheat raised *because the Lusitania was sunk*.

I go through the country and I see the smoke of many chimneys; where before there was only an arid plain, there is now a great city of 50,000 or 100,000 inhabitants reared almost in a day, and they are manufacturing night and day, *because the Lusitania was sunk*.

We see men going without food; without proper clothing; we see men everywhere stopping at noonday, praying that we may be victorious, and everywhere there is a spirit of fraternity, a determined spirit to help the weak and oppressed nations—why? *Because the Lusitania was sunk.*

You go across the sea and there the boys are going ashore, a hundred thousand a week, and they are over there to-day in the camps and in the trenches, *because the Lusitania was sunk.*

Two or three months ago Germany stood in such place of power that notwithstanding her suffering and hunger, she was sure to have won the World War if she had only been opposed by the English and the French. These nations were so worn out and so hungry themselves that they could not hope to defeat that great power and the war machinery which it had taken over fifty years to build up. The war would undoubtedly have been won by Germany, but *the Lusitania was sunk.* A great national crime was done. Consequently now millions of soldiers seem to be coming upon the shores rising from the sea, like some great phantom before Germany, and this makes it absolutely certain to any reasonable mind that Germany must soon seek for peace, and humbly seek for any kind of terms, that will let her

even have her own territory, *because the Lusitania
was sunk.*

O! no nation and no individual can hurl a sin
without its coming back again in after time. The sin
of the raids of the air and of the assassin submarines
is coming back to the German nation now. The
hand of God is used as an instrument to punish that
nation for its fearful sins; and no sin was greater in
the history of the world in all its wars than the sink-
ing of the *Lusitania.* Now every gun that is fired
will send its shells to kill the Germans and send
mourning into their homes. They say, and this is
conceded to be a very conservative estimate, that
300,000 Germans were killed during the last four
weeks. Think of 300,000 homes made dark and
black and sad for fifty years to come, *because the
Lusitania* was sunk. No sin can ever be committed
by individuals or by a nation but what its retribution will come, and hence I urge you, I warn you
that while you are choosing your life's profession,

"Choose life, that thou and thy seed may live!"

BENEDICTION

O Lord! Let the benediction of Thy care and
grace come upon our soldiers and sailors and nurses
wherever they are. May Thy benediction come
upon our nation, and give us a victory that will
bring a permanent peace and the brotherhood of all

mankind. Let Thy benedictions come upon the Philadelphia high school represented here, and may each member graduating come under Thine especial care. Let the benedictions of Thy love abide with us all evermore. Amen.

XI

The American Flag

(THE ACTS XXII : 28)

OUR Heavenly Father! we pray Thee this morning for the spirit which will guide our petitions so that we may pray in accord with the rules Thou hast laid down.

We pray Thee that Thou wilt take our nation under Thine especial care; we pray Thee that Thou wilt guide all of our affairs these important days, and that Thou wilt hinder anything that defeats the progress of righteousness and advance everything that tends toward good.

We know that our nation has sinned and fallen far short of Thy glory. We know that our people have gone into error, and wickedness, and that they have sinned. We know that we all deserve punishment from Thee. We know that we all need discipline from Thee. But O Lord we come to Thee asking Thee to forgive us as individuals and as a nation, and permit us to begin life anew under these circumstances, so that there will be no more mistakes made.

We pray that Thou wilt at this time come into the hearts of the people of this land, and be very close to them in this time of stress and excitement. Hold ever before them the cross of the Lord Jesus Christ, the Prince of Peace.

We pray Thee that Thou wilt keep our nation in a devout spirit, while determined to do its duty, yet ever preferring peace to war—always desiring those things that make for peace.

We pray that no opportunity shall pass in which peace might be secured without effort being strongly and sincerely made to secure it. We pray Thee that this war may close, and that it may be closed with the idea in the minds of men that patriotism is the patriotism of God; that it is the patriotism of the world; that it is the patriotism of humanity.

We pray Thee that all who worship Thee may keep close to the teachings of Thy Word; that they may realize that Christ is for all humanity. Help us to believe that humanity is larger than the United States; help us to realize that the whole world family is far more important than our local interests. Help us to look higher even than that—to recognize Thee as the King of Kings and the Lord of Lords—the only Ruler, O God! may our people never lose sight of that.

We pray Thee that this war, now upon us, may not take our people into savagery; that it may not take out of their hearts and lives the Christian principles given of Christ. We pray Thee that the Sabbath Day may still be respected; we pray Thee that the Bible may have free course in the hearts of the soldiers, and the sailors, and the home, and the Church. We pray Thee that the great principles of human liberty may prevail still.

O Lord! we pray Thee that the necessity for military life may not bring our people into harmony with autocracy, and monarchy, and tyranny, and dictatorship. We pray Thee that there may be maintained in our nation individual liberty of conscience, and as far as possible the individual liberty of every person's actions, and may the world see that we are still maintaining a pure and upright democracy, and be saved by the power of our example.

We ask that over the whole world there may soon come a time when all the people shall be brothers. We pray for the German people, and ask that soon they may be made to clearly understand that Christ is higher than Germany; we pray Thee that they may soon see that the Gospel applies as much to the world as it does to Germany, and we pray Thee that the same teachings may go to every other nation engaged in the war, and may all learn that our obligation to Thee is above every other obligation, and may America be noted, the world around, as being composed of sincere Christian men who believe in God, and who believe His laws are above all other laws, and whose service is above every other service. Lord, keep Thy Kingship and Thy power ever in front!

Hear our petition this morning for Thy blessing to be upon those who are serving our country. Hear us as we pray for Thy protecting care to be around our sailors and soldiers. Lord, guide them safely to victory.

Hear us as we pray for the suffering, and the sick, and those who are in great sorrow. Hear all our petitions, not for our much speaking, for Thou canst see our minds and read our thoughts—we ask all in the Name of Thy Son, the Lord Jesus Christ. Amen.

The text of to-night, about which I will speak a few minutes, is found in the 22d Chapter of Acts:

"And the chief captain answered, with a great sum I obtained this freedom. But Paul said, 'I was born free.'"

The first incident of childhood I can remember, and which I recall to-night, is that of frequent visits made to an old captain's home, who had served through the Revolutionary War. The old man would shoulder his crutch, march up and down the old New England kitchen, and tell us of the days of Bunker Hill, or Saratoga, or of Yorktown.

When we tried to question him, as little children would do, he would turn, and, with a fierce look of a war-god who would annihilate his little audience, exclaim, "What do you know about war? You were not born." The old man was proud of his gray hair, proud of the wounds he had received, proud of his crutches, proud of his pension. Old Captain Pomeroy was the valient hero of the whole neighborhood. What had we children to do with the War of the Revolution! We were not born!

They who fought in the Revolution bought our liberty with a great sum. They gave oh, so much for that which we now enjoy! It is unnecessary, before a reading and studious audience like this, for me to restate the great debts which cannot be calculated when we remind you how the forefathers served us, suffered for us, and died for us in the Revolution.

We have inherited the rich result of their deeds. We are enjoying without cost that which they purchased with blood. We are conscious of that. At the time when I was a small boy, we saw the generation of the Revolution pass over the border into the eternal beyond. But during the generation in which those soldiers lived, and those statesmen who had seen the Revoutionary days, wielded their power and wrought their patriotism into our form of government, they preserved carefully the principles for which they fought, and for which many of their comrades died.

Through their generation our liberty was safe. They had bought it with a great sum; they appreciated what it cost, and departure from the principles of liberty, of equality on the part of our government, and any attempt to use the flag of our nation to protect any person in any unrighteous undertaking, was immediately condemned by public sentiment by those who had seen war in its ravages. They whose homes had been burned, whose fields had been devastated, whose children had been torn on the field of battle, whose homes had been so desolate through the sad absence of father or brother, knew what it cost to win our liberty. While they lived, a firm hand was held upon every essential principle.

But we inherited without cost what they left us. The act of independence passed in this city was the declaration of brave men, who knew, as Franklin said, that they "must hang together or hang separately." They were brave men. We have said, perhaps, enough for this discussion concerning their bravery, their costly sacrifice.

The Declaration of Independence was signed on the Fourth of July, but the Act of Separation was passed by the Continental Congress on the second of July, in this, our patriotic city. We look back and find it was made possible by what God had done for this continent in the previous years. God had sent to Massachusetts the Pilgrim Fathers. He had sent to Rhode Island Roger Williams. God sent to Maryland Lord Baltimore. God sent to South Caroline Oglethorpe. He had sent John Wesley. He had sent the great pioneer martyrs, who gave their lives that Christianity might have a place of freedom in this fair land.

When this nation was born in yonder hall, it was but the outcome, the concrete result, of a previous religious training. A nation founded upon the Bible, the Rock Jesus Christ, came into existence, and those Christian principles given by the love of God, in the Bible teachings were maintained through the first generation of our nation's existence.

We look back with surprise upon what so few people—only three millions, accomplished. But when you of my age came upon this world we came like Paul; we were born into this noble condition. We inherited what our forefathers had left to us. We could not say, with our proud Roman captain, "I bought this freedom with a great price." We could not say we had engaged in any long war, or that we gave our sons or husbands; we could not say that we risked all that we might be free and our children might enjoy liberty. But we could say with Paul, "I was born free."

To be able to say, "I was born free" and appreciate the inheritance, was something so remarkable that it placed Paul even above the Roman centurion, for he who inherits privileges usually values them at the least. Such was the case from 1840 to 1860. From 1840 to 1860, the generation that was born into this glorious inheritance forgot what it cost. They had inherited it in the second generation only, and did not appreciate its value, just as a young man or woman now inherits a great fortune. They know not how hard the father or mother worked, or how intently they saved or sacrificed to get together that property, and they spend it uselessly or in riotous living. We find that from 1840 to 1860 this nation went on rioting with its inheritance, forgot its value, and increased more and more its tendency toward slavery, until the stars and stripes, under a new generation, represented a nation that enslaved four million of people, and the nation, by its legislative acts, by its armies, by its presidency, had forgotten the Declaration of Independence, which said that all mankind are born free and endowed with certain inalienable rights to life, liberty and the pursuit of happiness.

What a contradiction it was—the flag of the free in 1860! Then we had to fight over again the battle of 1776. We were compelled to make the flag what our forefathers claimed it must be, namely, the flag of the free. We were obliged to make great sacrifices then, and as I look back through the years I see the blue lines of regiments hurrying into battle. I hear them tramping on now. I can see the awful contest, I hear the thunder strokes of the cannon, the hiss of the bullets. I see the flash of the swords and bayonets; see the ground covered with the dead; hear the groans, and again we carry off the battle-fields during the long night, the suffering and dying. O! liberty costs a great sum.

Then 1865 came, and the million of men—North and South—who returned to their homes once more could all say, "This is the flag of the free, and by a good sum we have purchased this freedom." Then for a score of years this land was held to freedom. From 1860 to 1880 this land, through the influence of the soldiers of the nation, was held strictly accountable for every unpatriotic act, and steadily and surely liberty held up her light before the world, supported on every side with the hands that had given something for their freedom, and were ready to give much more.

Millions of men were scattered over this land who had faced cannon, who had felt its smoke in their eyes, and heard the hiss of its shot in their ears, or who had fallen and lain bleeding on the battlefield. Such men had purchased their freedom and purchased it with a great price. They understood its value and the flag was the flag of the free.

It was during that score of years, following 1865, that this nation had more influence over the other nations of the earth than throughout all its history. From 1865 to 1875, only ten years, it gave parts of its constitution to seventeen different nations, who, imitating our example of freedom, copied our laws and adopted our institutions. During that twenty years Europe saw three of her great nations copying our form and advocating our ideas of liberty. Even the heathen in distant lands, and especially Japan, copied us in our example, our teachings, our schools, our voting system, our colleges, our academies, our science, our improvements. During that twenty years when men lived who had seen the cost of liberty and understood its value, this nation needed no army, no navy to win the respect of mankind. Then, if it uttered its fiat or expressed its opinion, the nations of Europe respected it.

But a nation has arisen born into this liberty and being born into it, do they appreciate it as Paul did, or do they not? I find that the nation in the last thirty years has gradually been taken aside from the patriotic position it held in 1865, until now great dangers arise. I do not anticipate great losses. I am not one of those who look upon this nation in such a fearful exigency. It cannot go far back. But I am one of those among the old men of the generation now left behind, who cannot fail to warn you that the history of the past is likely to be repeated. If it is repeated, there will come to this generation the time when your freedom will again cost you much.

We come to this generation which has come into that power and say that we have the old flag with us. We have seen it in battle; we have seen it go down before a brave foe; we have seen it raised by brave heroes, who fell in lifting that flag again and again. The older we grow the more awful it seems, and the closer becomes the comradeship of the Grand Army of the Republic. We have seen it, we know its cost.

We cannot impress it upon this generation as we would; but we commit the flag to you. It represents what our forefathers fought for in the Revolution; it represents the bloody feet of Valley Forge; it represents the great sacrifices of Washington; it represents the bravery of John Hancock and John Adams; it represents the oratory of Patrick Henry and Daniel Webster; it represents the grand patriotism of Henry Wilson, of Douglas, of Lincoln, of Garrison and of Wendell Phillips. It represents all the oratory, all the patriotism, all the battles, all the fighting of 1861 to 1865. It represents the graves of men and the tears of women. It means much to the soldier who fought for it. We commit it to your care, and we ask you to remember that it represents "personal liberty."

Do you think that in 1865 or in 1870 a mob could have burned at the stake a negro in Georgia? Do you think it could have been done while soldiers of the North and of the South—a million of them—still lived in this land? But now you hear of it and forget it. The Indians who preceded us here, who burned their captives at the stake, resorted to no such hideous cruelty as now sometimes comes under this flag, untried and uncondemned in some of the States.

O friends, we leave you this flag! But shall it go on meaning that law shall not be respected, or shall every man, whether he be black or white, be allowed an honest trial, and have the right to defend his innocence, and shall every man be condemned who doth wrong? Shall savages or true men have the care of womanhood committed to them? Shall that be its future? We have seen the day when the flag meant that no man, white or black, could be condemned without an honest trial. We have seen it. Will you see it again? Will you, who have taken this flag from us, carry it on in that old way, and bravely declare that wherever that flag flies every man shall have an honest trial, and the mandates of the law shall be promptly executed?

This flag means a right to free organization. But

we see it shelter now great combinations that are injurious to our interests. We see great trusts formed now, which, by the fearful force of capital, are taking your liberty from you and from your children, and raising up a moneyed aristocracy that would rule the land instead of the people. Instead of a government of the people, by the people and for the people, it is in danger of becoming a government of the few.   ,

Four hundred and eighty families own forty-one per cent. of all the property in this land now, and if all those families chose to combine, with their great money power, they could erect an aristocracy that would rule this land. This land could become an empire, even here where our children enjoy this liberty! Let us begin to appreciate this inheritance. If it costs us blood; if it costs us all the terrible sacrifices of a war of 1776, or 1812, or 1861, there will be no danger from these trusts. But a generation has been born into this condition, and does not yet appreciate what it cost.

We believe that a man, or a set of men, has the right, under our constitution and our liberty, to organize with their capital. All trusts are not bad. Many trusts are for the good of the people, and all trusts ought to be for the good of the people. The laws of the land ought also to protect the liberty of the individual to such an extent that no combinations could deprive him of his honest rights. And that day must come, but it may cost you much. It will cost you blood, cost you loss of treasure, cost you perhaps loss of liberty unless you appreciate what the flag means.

The flag means that all men shall have the right to organize but never the right to so combine as to deprive any individual of his natural rights. We are accusing the trusts a great deal more than we ought. I believe that we ought to sustain some of them, as I cannot see how our liberty or prosperity can be preserved without them.

The greatest trust on earth is the association of working men. There is no trust so great as these organizations of working men. I would not have the right taken away from them. The right to combine their capital and their labor into one great trust should not be taken away. If you take it away from the working men, you must take it away from the incorporated companies or take it away from the capitalists. But the flag represents the theory that every individual under its folds has an equal right to an opportunity to succeed in life. We will need now to utter these principles again to the world, that men shall not combine to enslave their fellow-men, whether it be in an autocracy or in large trusts of capital, or trusts of labor organizations, for the principles apply fully to them all.

Will the next Fourth of July be celebrated by the mere lighting of fire crackers or exhibition of games, entirely forgetful that on this day the nation was born, and ignoring the importance of teaching again the principles of liberty and righteousness according to the commandment of God.

In a large part of this land the Fourth of July has become only a holiday for sports; and when they have finished the day, and if they are catechized concerning the Declaration of Independence or the Constitution of the United States, or what the Fourth of July stands for, they will only be able to answer you in terms of baseball. You cannot to-day expect all of these people, who thus celebrate the Fourth of July to rightly value what they have inherited. But God asks us now to buy our freedom with a great sum.

The flag represents universal peace among the nations. It is not a war flag. It means something better than war. Our flag does not mean war. It never did mean destruction. It has meant a building up always. This flag never represented the savagery of war. Any man can tear down. The devil delights in destruction. Any man can girdle a tree that has seen a slow growth of a century. Any man can with a match burn down a building that has cost a million of dollars. It takes a grand, noble and great nation to rise and build up and make beautiful the architecture of the world, and to make great souls of men, and to guide them toward heaven. That is what the flag means.

This flag does stand for a permanent universal peace, for upbuilding, for fraternity all over the earth. Will it stand so to those who have inherited it? Will it always mean that those states which agreed to form a nation in 1780, made a compact for all time, and will it mean that all states who join our national family must do so as volunteers?

This flag means sympathy always with the oppressed. I have often thought of that night when the President in 1848 arose from his bed on receiving a despatch from Daniel Manin, at Venice, and ordered that recognition of independence of the Venician Republic should be sent on the very next ship to the little Republic approving their attempt to make themselves free from the tyranny of Austria. That was true patriotism. That represented what the people mean that there is no nation on earth so low, so poor or so small, but that if it be groveling under hard tyranny it has the sympathy of the hearts of all our people. There is not a scene of carnage in Armenia but what awakens a throb of sympathy in the United States, and our flag is a protest against the tyranny of the Turkish government.

There is not a case of slavery in Africa, not a

hideous murder in South America, but what has the
moral protest of the lines upon our flag, and has
the condemnation of the stars that shine in its blue.
The flag means sympathy with the oppressed where-
ever they may be, and under the light this land is
an asylum for the oppressed.

Not an Armenian finds his way from the shores
of Palestine but should be welcomed from the heart
of the people to the shores of America.   There is
not a person oppressed in Russia among the Jewish
people, but what finds a hearty welcome when he
reaches our shores.   We are sometimes burdened
by the incoming of some classes, but the hearts of
the American people have been opened all the years
to the incoming of the oppressed of every land.
This is still the land of the free.

Whenever a foot touches this shore it is free and
it is welcomed.   Whoever cometh to this land to
make his home, whoever cometh here to escape from
tyranny, whoever cometh here to grow more intelligent or more moral, or to love God better, is welcome.   That is what the flag means—what it has
meant through the years.   But in these later days
there had grown up a selfish spirit in the generation
that has inherited what cost the fathers so much,
and a tendency was seen to shut out by law the poor
and suffering people who would find a home of rest
in our beloved land.   But the flag means an open

welcome. Make it mean so in future years. Pay the price.

The flag means that this is the land of the fully free—every person free—each one having the exercise of his natural rights. O, ye men who have inherited all this priceless treasure, would you extend it for the good of your fellowmen! Won't you be sure that there arises no power, whether it be the money power or political power, that shall enslave our people; that shall make the many serve the few? Won't you preserve this government in these dangerous days so that the people themselves still shall rule? Won't you beware of political combinations that give any one man permanent power over thousands of people? Won't you beware of any combination of capital that makes one man a king over thousands in this land? Won't you beware of any combination that gives states or cities or towns authority to control the individuals by some corporate power? Won't you beware that all people, white or black, rich or poor, shall all be equal before the law? Let us live the character at home we would fight for in the field.

It is necessary that you preserve your judiciary with the greatest care. It is necessary to see that your laws are enforced with precision. It is necessary that the criminal is ever condemned and that the innocent ever goes free. It is necessary to help the poor that they may have an equal chance with the rich.

A person born in this land in late years without money has been at a disadvantage where the laws of the state and the people did not extend a helping hand to him as a child, and give him an opportunity to obtain an education, an opportunity to secure a trade, or an opportunity to be independent of that condition which would place him in the chains of poverty.

If you would still keep this the land of the free you must extend Christian principles. Don't shut the Bible out of your schools. Don't take the Bible out of your courts. Don't forget the Sabbath Day. Don't forget the Ten Commandments, for those principles God has taught and Christianity has taught has made this country what it is. Carry these principles out for the sake of the price they cost in the days gone by, and value them so justly as to pay unhesitatingly another instalment on the great sum our peaceful homes, our equality and freedom are worth. May the God of nations accept the price we offer.

XII

Harvest Home

(GENESIS 1 :12)

TO-NIGHT, as I appeal to the Sunday School scholars, I wish to preach seven sermons. First, upon the text, "Each Seed After His Own Kind." I take in my hand two different articles, which I have picked up from this heap of harvest products. What kind of a seed do you suppose was planted to produce that tomato? Do you suppose that if you planted this egg-plant that the tomato would grow from it? If you planted an onion would it come up a cabbage? If you planted wheat would it come up rye? If you planted a pepper would it come up an apple tree? So find another text, "Whatsoever a man soweth that shall he also reap." If a boy or girl in life, should sow bad thoughts or sinful actions, such a boy or girl will reap what they sow. Whatsoever a man soweth that shall he also reap. That is my first sermon.

My second sermon is drawn from this tree. Do you suppose that this tree in the field was all above ground? Here are some oak bushes. How much of that tree do you suppose is under ground? More of it perhaps under ground than above ground. The roots are running far out underneath, further than the limbs extend out into the air, although the roots do not extend as far down into the ground as the branches extend into the air. What is the reason for that? It evidently was God's intention when He arranged that a tree should grow, that it should derive its nourishment from the air and the ground, but mostly from the air, but the roots are placed down underneath. While they do serve a helpful purpose towards the sustenance of the tree, yet there is some other great design. Why do the roots run so far out under ground? Why are they made so strong, like iron cables in strength? It is because somewhere, in the course of that tree's life, there are going to be storms; and when that wind comes from the mountains or the cyclone sweeps over the plains and strikes this tree it will stand firm if its roots run wide under ground. There is a boy here. He is a pretty good boy now, but the roots of his religious character have perhaps not been placed far enough under ground; he has not been planted deep enough in settled character so that when another boy comes along with some temptation he goes over with the storm or in the time of excitement or anger he falls. Many a man goes over because in his youth his character was not founded deep enough, strong enough and wide enough to hold him in place.

Another thought also comes in connection with the tree: If I hang a weight upon this branch—take this sickle and hang it on this tree, and if this were a growing tree, that weight on that limb would, after a while, cause it to stay in that bent position, and when it grew up to be a great tree it would still bow like that. I remember an apple tree very distinctly, that grew on the hillside back of our house, and whenever, as a boy, I came in from the harvest field, I would run along the top of the hill as fast as I could and swing from one of those branches, swinging away down the hill and bending the branch over every time. I was at the old farm last week and there is that tree bent over to the ground where I bent it when I was a boy. As the twig is bent so the tree is inclined, and if a boy or girl in youth contracts any bad habits those habits are very sure to remain to hinder them all through life.

It is curious how we are bound down by habit. Every man finds himself doing things that he did when a boy, and somehow is not able to overcome those habits. I saw a minister the other day who was in the habit of thrusting both hands in his pockets when he was preaching. I asked him why it was and he said, "I am fighting that habit all the time; my wife and daughter call my attention to it and I have thought of having my pockets sewed up to prevent it. But I got into the habit when I was a boy and somehow cannot get out of it." As that little habit afflicted him so there are habits that afflict all of us—habits contracted when we were young. When a boy falls into bad company and does those things in his youth that he will be sorry for when he is old he will drop into these bad habits without knowing it.

I recall a minister who was a very good preacher. But one day I heard him swear. I felt shocked to hear a preacher of the gospel of Jesus Christ using profane language, and afterwards when I spoke to him about it he said, "It was the first time that I have given way since I became a Christian. But that overcame me, I was so angry that I fell into the old habit before I could command myself." It is dangerous, even after you become a Christian—these habits will come out.

I want to preach another sermon. I wonder if there are any heads of wheat here. When a tree or stalk bends because it is loaded with fruit it is a beautiful thing. How much would you give for a field of wheat whose stalks stood up straight like that? You would not give anything for it. Why is it that some people go around with their heads so high in the air, looking above the heads of their fellowmen. It is because there is nothing in their heads. There is nothing there to hold the head down. When a head of wheat is heavy it bends over. When you see a man who is a thoroughly godly man, whose brain is skilled and who is a great genius, his head bends over. Not that he is round shouldered, but he is a modest man. When Jesus Christ spoke of the merit of humility when He taught us to remember that God was over all and that we were weak and sinful, He taught us that great truth illustrated by the wheat. As soon as religion enters into our hearts our heads will reverently bow.

Now I have here a number of leaves. Those leaves are the lungs of the tree. Like men, they give out something and they take in something with every breath. They build up the tree and the tree is simply made up of the bark that has grown every year. There is a great tree in England that is more than three thousand years old. By boring into it they have found more than three thousand rings or layers of bark. So the great tree of to-day is only its past self covered by outer bark. Now the character of a boy or girl is simply the accumulated experience of the various years. Year by year we increase in a bad character or a good character. But as to these leaves—they are of great use. It is said that we could not live for more than nine minutes if it were not for trees, because the leaves give out the oxygen which is necessary for our life. They take

in the poisonous stuffs from the air and give out
healthful oxygen. That is the reason why a forest
is such a beautiful place, because there are so many
leaves giving out oxygen. If you can get into a
forest, where there are not to many decaying leaves,
it is the healthiest place in the world.

I have looked all around here since I have been
on the platform and I cannot find a single weed.
That is unnatural. A weed or two would have made
this decoration seem more realistic. At least it would
to every farmer's boy, like myself. My back has
ached and my feet have smarted and I have worked
until the perspiration has dropped from my forehead
over these weeds. The weeds multiply faster than
the grain. You plant a little grain of wheat and it
multiplies thirty, sixty or a hundred fold—that is,
you get back one hundred grains for every one you
plant. But if you plant a sunflower, which is a
dreadful weed in some places, it produces two thousand seeds for one. If you plant a thistle, that always bears at least four thousand seeds. It is so
easy to plant a weed and it is so easy for it to multiply. It is so easy for us to plant an action that
is wrong, it is so easy to sow a word that is bad.
You see lots of boys who would rather use slang
than decent language. You hear boys say "Gee,"
which is a cowardly way of saying "Jesus." Yet
they try, by such weak, little, contemptible methods,

to sneak behind swearing. Don't be a contemptible sneak and hide behind the bush, to throw stones. Bad words are so easy to use and good words are so commonplace, it would seem. Words and actions are like plants—bad actions are like the thistle but good actions are like the wheat. It is so much easier to tear down than to build up. The destroyers are frequent, the builders are rare.

I have here an ear of corn. It had to be protected by this husk while it was young. If it had not stayed in that husk it would never have been the perfect ear that it is to-day. And so the child in the home must be protected by mother's care and father's power and be kept in the shade. The child may say, "I do not like to be kept at home and tied to my mother's apron strings and obey my father." But the boy who does not do so will never grow up into perfect manhood and form his character as he ought to form it. The home-nest is the place for the boy until the time comes for him to take his place in the world and do his own duty. Children who do not stay at home become blighted ears and covered with mildew. That is what happens to the corn if it is exposed to the air before the proper time.

Then I come to my next sermon, and that is that this ear of corn can do a wonderful thing for you. Now you boys and girls go to school. Suppose you take just one kernel of corn and plant it and it always produces a hundred fold? How long would it take to plant the whole of the arable land of the world with Indian corn from that one kernel? It would take only five years. And if every Christian would sow a kernel of good deeds how long would it take to win the world to Christ? If every Christian in this church or Sunday School were to sow one good deed or bring one soul to Christ each year and those thus brought to Christ were to do likewise, it would not be twenty-five years before the whole world would be Christian. What a lesson is taught us by the corn when we think that in five years, from one single grain we could cover the earth with Indian corn.

Do you know that all the fruits were once wild? Do you know that the tomato was called a ground persimmon; that it was very puckery and would draw your mouth all up so that you could hardly get your lead pencil in? The great-great grandfather of the pepper was a little weedy thistle that grew in the southern part of India. The celery you eat was so poisonous that a single stalk of it would have killed any man only a very few years ago. Do you know what was the great, great, great grandfather of the pear? If you will go into the mountains you will see the mountain ash, having red berries on it, not larger than a pea. It is a pretty tree, but if you ever tasted those berries you would not call it a luscious tree. I remember once having been deceived by a man who told me they were currants. I took a handful and put them into my mouth at once and spit them out very quickly. Yet that bitter red berry is the great grandfather of the Bartlett pear. Perhaps some of you children may have heard of Burbank, who has been taking the great cacti of the desert and grafting them so as to change their nature, and they have become luscious food for the animals. I know that on our farm there grew a thorn bush. Well do I remember its prickles. But one day a man came from Boston and he grafted a pear twig on that thorn bush and last summer I walked over to the meadow and that bush was full of pears. The fruit tree had covered the thorn tree altogether. All our grains have come from something wild in the past. Even the carrots and the potatoes were once wild. Every fruit and vegetable on this platform has come from wild ancestors. Just as the boys and girls start in life wild. I have seen wild boys, and some of them live not very far from here. I have seen wild girls, and some of them live in this neighborhood. Indeed, all boys would be wild Indians or worse if they were not cultivated and cared for and taught. Every child must have a character grafted .into it—must have Christ's character added in order to have a character worthy of heaven. The pear tree and the apple tree are no more the product of the original thorn than is the Christian the product of the original vicious and sinful nature with which he is born.

All that is worth having cost something in care; and these boys and girls have had the sufferings of father and mother, and have been an expense to their parents and source of great anxiety and care. If they have good and noble characters to-day they should remember that it is the result of watching and careful prayer and labor of father and mother. The boy or girl who does not appreciate the sacrifices of parents has not approached the line of a Christian character. I would like these boys and girls to go to their homes from this anniversary with the thought in their minds, "I am going to be a Christian, I am going to try and serve Christ, and I will begin by being obedient to my father and mother.

Then, think how all the leaves must die in order to live. If you planted a diamond or an emerald, would it grow? If you planted a stone, would it grow? Everything that lives must die to live on. Nothing which cannot die can ever live. Now this corn is the product of corn that is dead—corn that died in the ground and reproduced itself in this, the resurrection. Every kind of fruit tree, every sort of grain has gone continually through that death and resurrection period. Therefore, remember this, that every one must die in order to live again. A stone cannot die and therefore it does not rise to a new life. A man cannot live again unless he dies. So that my lesson is that every fruit around us here is an assurance of the resurrection. Some previous fruit died that this might live; my ancestors died that I might live, so it is only through death that we reach the better things in the progress of our spiritual life. Not a pear would be fit to eat if it had not been for many previous fruits dying and thus reproducing themselves in better form, and it is owing to those previous deaths that the pear is now the luscious fruit that it is. And so he who would enter heaven and live hereafter must die—descend bodily into the ground that he may rise again to resurrection life beyond. Children, you and I must die, but that death, as we call it, is only a way leading to something better. It is nothing to look upon with gloom and sadness. If we believe in Jesus Christ, if we have trusted Him as our Saviour, we need not fear the grave or death, whether it comes early or late, because it is only the transition from the poor, bitter, miserable fruit into the lovely, blooming fruitage of an existence that shall be eternal.

BENEDICTION

And now may the benediction of God so descend upon these services that we will never forget that he who goeth forth with weeping bearing precious seed shall doubtless come again rejoicing and bringing his sheaves with him.   Grant, O God, such a benediction of Thy spirit upon this thought and upon this people that we shall go out to reap, and wilt Thou make it sure that somewhere in time or eternity we shall see the "harvest home."   We ask that benediction in the Master's name.   Amen.

XIII

"Go Forward"—A Rally Day Sermon

(EXODUS XIV:15)

*A*ND the Lord said unto Moses, wherefore cryest thou unto me. Speak unto the children of Israel and tell them to go forward."

We put our hands into the hands of the Lord this morning and say: "Lord, lead on, we are ready." As a church, we cease from our Summer wanderings. We turn our attention to the great duties that confront us and we say, "Lord, here we are! Send us!" And the Lord sayeth unto us as He said unto the children of Israel, "Go Forward." He will never say to us, "Sit down by the shore and wait." He will never say to us so long as sin is in the world, "Rest here in peace." But with each recurring year, with the beginning of each undertaking, He sayeth unto us, "Go forward!" He did not say to the children of Israel that they were to cease offering up their supplications, but He said, "Why do you ask my advice and then refuse to take it. It is time you went forward." Moses said, "Here is the sea with its wild billows raging, beating on the shore. We cannot go forward." But again the voice comes down from the highest dome of heaven's temple, saying, "Go forward!" But Moses sayeth, "Here is the sea; there are the mountains; behind us the enemy. We are surrounded on every side with a wall of difficulties. Lord, what are we to do!" Again comes the voice, "Go forward."

So to-day the voice comes to you and to me, "Go Forward!" We sometimes long to be in a land of rest, and we say, "There is a rest for the people of God," but it is over on the other side of the river. We sometimes declare, "Oh, when we have finished this thing, we will sit down and rest." But as soon as that thing is done, God says, "No, not now! Do something else." So He says to you the same thing.

"You have been looking forward to the time when we would get the debt on the Church paid and you have thought, "Then we will rest in quietness and peace under our own vine and fig tree." But the Lord says, "No, if you sit down, the Egyptians are behind you, the immovable waves are before you, the only thing to do is to put your feet into the water," as He afterward commanded them in the River Jordan.

I visited the seashore, and finding the life-saving station closed, I inquired for some person who could show me the apparatus. They told me a farmer back on the farm had the key. The farmer said

that some months ago a yacht had put out from the
harbor with a company of people on it, among them
his brother. After they had been out a while, there
came a severe squall which overturned the yacht and
threw the people into the water. But all managed to
cling to the riggings, sails or spars. In that terrible gale the sea beat over them and buried them for
a moment with the coming tidal wave. The farmer
was at his house watching the boat, and he ran down
to the shore to see what could be done to help them.
As the boat overturned, its long mast stuck in the
sand and anchored the boat, so that every wave drove
the mast deeper into the sand. The farmer went
down and tried to get into the life-saving station.
He had no key but at last he broke into the window
and opened the door. He found there a great mortar, or a kind of a gun, into which they put a bomb
or shot which they fire into the sky that it may fall
beyond the vessel, and the line attached to it come
within reach of those who are perishing. But he
was a farmer. What did he know about artillery?
What did he know about a life-saving station? A
little farther in, he found an immense apparatus
upon wheels that could be turned easily. It had a
great many ropes, some anchors and many pulleys,
and he anxiously ran around that and wished to
know what that was for. But there was no person
to tell him. He pulled at the ropes and cogs and

tried to separate the ropes. Then he found a number of life preservers, one of them on wheels. He examined them, but here they were, far back from the shore and his friends were out in the ocean, perhaps drowning even then. Here was all the apparatus to save them. The Government had expended many thousands of dollars for that purpose. But he did not know how to use it or what to do with it. He did not dare put any powder into that mortar or fire it. He did not dare run the wheels of that machine into the sea. He simply stood and trembled, and cried on the shore, and his brother went down into the sea, and his body was washed up when the storm was gone. This helpless man stood crying, surrounded by everything that was needed to save every person on that boat. We are in that same position ourselves. All around us as a Church, men are going down; all about us are the sick and suffering; all around us the ignorant; on every side the need of sympathy, of kindness, of Christian love; and we, with a mighty life-saving station, with all the ropes and cogs, with all the bombs and shells, stand and tremble, and cry, and do nothing. Yet we are life-savers. Your Church is composed of three-fourths young people, in their strength and prime, with all the ambitions and hopes. It is a great life-saving station. Your Church has in it the energy of active business men. It is composed of the middle class of the community; not the absolutely poor, or the greatly wealthy. It is a great life-saving station. You have the public favor of the city. Never did a church receive such great kindness, such voluntary support, such help from public opinion, from the public press and from society as seem to gather around you. A great life-saving station is here with everything ready to work, with all the men and women to use it. But men are dying still. People are in awful pain and suffering because no hand reaches them. Thousands are going into sin and crime because no Christian sympathizes with them. If this were the only church in the city, our responsibility would not be any greater than now.

If each member of the Church were to give ten cents a week toward foreign missions,—what a power for good that would be! If each member of the Chorus were to sing one soul into the Kingdom, that would be 3,000 people converted by them every year, if they only converted one a month. Suppose each usher were to make a friend of one stranger each Sunday, that one would multiply to 1,560 strangers made friends of the Church in a year. If the attendants of the Societies of the Church were to convert one soul a month, they would convert 60,000 people in one year in this Church. Well may we talk of the responsibility upon individual Christians. Suppose each one of us should visit a sick person, as Jesus went around visiting the sick. If each person in this Church visited only one a week, this Church alone would reach 130,000 suffering people in a year. I feel small when I think of the power of God that has dwelt in your midst. God says, "Go Forward," and we are going. No place in this Church for lazy people any more. No place in this community for those who will not do their duty. We are for God. We are for humanity. We are for the sick, for the sinful; we are for the whole city. We are to save them all.

Did you ever think of your power with God in prayer? It is a dangerous thing to have such power with God. It makes you fearfully responsible for the manner in which you use it, for the petitions you make and for the things you pray for. You have great business force. I do not believe a member of the Church should lend money to another member of the Church and regard it as a kindness. It is no kindness to go around lending money. There is nothing on earth that makes a man hate you so much as to know he owes you money. The obligation of the Church is on a wider, higher plane. Its obligation is that every member of the Church has something to do, and it is our duty to see that no member of the Church is ever out of work, and if you know of a position at a good salary and you know of a member occupying a place at a smaller salary, it is your privilege and duty to try and help that member. You have wonderful business power in the city, reaching out into 32 professions and into 82 kinds of business, many of you connected with the most important enterprises of the city. Throughout the whole city you have this effective social force. How are we going to use these forces? What are we going to do this coming Fall and Winter with these social and spiritual machines?

During the Civil War, down below Chatanooga, the General came to one of the Massachusetts regiments and said, "I want to see if there are men in this regiment who can fix up this railroad so we can run a freight train over it by next Thursday. I have orders from General Sherman, and he wants it by next Thursday?" We were all called out, and the General came down the line and said, "What can YOU do?" One man said, "I never worked on a railroad, but I can drive spikes." The General said, "Step out; you can drive spikes!" Each of them knew something, and between them they knew about the whole railroad business. The General divided them up and said, "This man can take charge of this, and you of that. You go to work on the rails, and you on this engine, and you on that," and every man said, "I will do my part!" The next Thursday afternoon the great freight train went toward Dallas, Georgia, and when the troops came in, so hungry, oh, what a delight it was to see them rolling out the biscuits and the pickles! Although no man knew the whole business, each man in his own place did his duty right there. We as a Church, have this great machine. We have this life-saving station. We have these people to save. God has given us apparatus of all kinds and forms. No one knows how to control the whole machine, but each of us knows how to do something, and there are enough of us here, so that with us all, we know all about it. God says, "Go Forward," and if we are to go forward from this Rally Day on, each member of the Church must do his own individual duty in his own place, drive the spikes or repair the engine. God calls to you from the sky and says, "Why cryest thou unto me? Say unto Israel, Go Forward." You cannot escape the awful responsibility God has placed upon you in this Church.

I could pray God sincerely that I had a small church; that I was back in the country town in a small church. I could pray God sincerely at this hour that God would let me retire to some place where there were few people and where the great interests of the community were not so tied to the on-going machine of a great church. I could ask Him to shift this responsibility to some better hands and stronger minds. But we cannot escape. Our shoulders are under the building; it will fall unless you and I lift it, and if you lift, and I lift, it will not be a difficult undertaking. We may not be able to rest this side of glory, but we will feel that we have not been cowards or deserters. Lord, we put our hands again in Thine. Go ON! We are ready to follow. We will do what we can.

XIV

Thanksgiving Sacrifice

(PSALMS CVII :22)

MY text this morning is in the 107th Psalm and the 22d verse:

"Let them sacrifice the sacrifices of thanksgiving and declare His works with rejoicing."

The sacrifice of thanksgiving, under the Old Testament dispensation, was an offering of something that was valuable to the owner. It was a sheep or a bullock that would have brought a high price in the market. And the thanksgiving offerings made in those days were made from the very best they had, and were voluntary offerings, or free will, and, unlike many other offerings, it was not required to be made at stated seasons. The thank offering was made whenever a man felt disposed to do it. It was a free-will offering, of his own accord, made at a time when he felt especially thankful to the Lord. Then he brought the best of his flocks and offered it unto the Lord. Other offerings were systematic and were made at stated intervals throughout the year in the Temple. It was an offering they made just before a feast. If a man had occasion to give a great feast; if his family had been well married; if a son had been born in the family; if a great blessing in the way of business prosperity had reached him,—then he gave a feast and invited his friends. But before he sat down at the feast he carried to the temple, or sent, a thank offering, being unwilling to feast himself until he had first thanked God for the blessings which led to the feast.

Now the text, which I cannot present to-day as it should be presented, has within it a spiritual idea which Christ evidently sought to evolve from it. When Jesus abolished the Old Testament system He did not do away with the spirit of the law. He discontinued these thank offerings in the form of sheep or bullocks, but He came to fulfil in the spirit what was done before in the letter. He did not abolish our thanksgiving offering; on the contrary, He enforced the spirit of it. You remember how He told His disciples that when they brought their gifts to the altar, if they remembered that they had aught against another, or he against them, they were to go first and be reconciled with that brother, and then offer the gift. It enforced the same spirit which was supposed to be behind the Old Testament provision.

Then, when Jesus was describing the final judgment, He said, "Inasmuch as ye have done it unto the least of these, my brethren, ye have done it unto

me." We were to still worship God and to make
thank offerings, but the way we were to express our
thanksgiving was to do some deed of helpfulness to
these, His brethren, on the earth. He simply
changed the form and not the spirit of the thanksgiving offering.

We have come to this Thanksgiving week in the
history of our lives, and we ask ourselves, "What is
it to be religiously thankful? What ought we to
do?" In this text we have this express command,
"Let them sacrifice the sacrifice of thanksgiving."
If we are to sacrifice, let us do it now, before we
feast.

One of the dear old Quakers of your own state,
of whom I read with interest years ago, always went
to his Thanksgiving dinner by the way of a little
side room, where he knelt for a few moments in
prayerful thanksgiving and put in a small box the
amount to a cent which the Thanksgiving dinner
had cost him and his family. Then was his conscience clear; then was he comforted by the thought
that he had made his sacrifice offering to God, and
he went to this simple, plain feast of the Friends
with a delight, and a joy of soul, peace of mind, and
rest of body such as another could not have known.
Jesus taught the principle that it was right to feast,
but that we were to go to that feast by the way of
sacrifice.

O my friends! how few people thank the Lord! How few really good men there are in this world! There are half-good ones! There are half-hearted ones! There are half-learned ones, but how few come up to the utmost standard of what Christ sets here as possible. How few true offerings there are, and how sacred are these few! It is a very curious thing that the Lord makes ten thousand millions of seeds for every one tree that grows from the seed, and so He makes ten thousand human beings in order to get one real man. It seems a very curious thing that He should have wasted (apparently to us, but not to Him) His strength, that there should be so few real sacrifices made, so few real men, full men, complete men, out of all the millions that the Lord brings into being.

How many trees there are! If any of you own a farm, you have found out how many trees grow there which bear no fruit. You have about six trees to one apple, as a rule, nowadays. The trees grow where you don't want them, all around, by the fence and on the roads. You have all the trees, but when you go out in the Fall season and ought to find fruit, you find only here and there an apple, only here and there a tree that bears fruit. So many men there are in the world who are supposed to bear fruit, but so few actually bear the fruit for which they are intended. How many of us have prayed and prayed that we might be counted among those who are worthy to be esteemed His disciples, and yet there are only a sacred few. Christ Himself said to His disciples, "Pray the Lord of the harvest that He send laborers into his vineyard." "The harvest surely is plentiful, but the laborers are few," Jesus said to them. When there were already hundreds of Christian human beings on the earth, Jesus said to them, "The laborers indeed are few."

How few make the sacrifice of thanksgiving during this Thanksgiving week in its best form! How many express their gratitude to God beyond words and prayers! Now, this is Thanksgiving week. We profess to be thankful. We praise God and thank Him for His mercies untold, but what fruit do we bear? Why, we grow up in the spring, we put on our green leaves, and we spread forth our blossoms of thanksgiving, but when this week is gone and God asks us, "Where is the fruit?" we must answer, "There is no fruit!" All the flowers blasted! Nothing but words! Nothing but form! No offerings, no real sacrifice to God!

Once in a while I hear of some heroic deed in connection with my life work in educating or helping to educate young men. I heard of one who gave me a high opinion of a young man's gratitude. An old farmer in New Hampshire assisted this young man to go to Harvard College, and when he had finished his course in Harvard he desired to go to Europe. He secured a scholarship which would have paid his tuition in one of the great universities of Europe. His goods were packed and he had procured his ticket to sail, when he heard that the dear old farmer was very sick and his crops were ready for the harvest. When he heard the facts, that the farmer was sick and that the harvest was ready on that farm in New Hampshire, where it was so difficult to obtain help, he returned his ticket at a discount and took a train for the farm. Although he had been a student all his life, he went right out in the clothes of a farmer and harvested the crops during that season. When the next Spring time came he had an opportunity again, for they always come to such men as these, and he went to Europe with a brighter view, a lighter heart and an ambition purified and blessed indeed by the offering he made to that old benefactor. This young man was sufficiently appreciative of what his benefactor had done for him to go there and actually gather his crops under the heated sun, exposing himself for the benefactor. We all honor a man who will do that. Of course that man will go to the highest places! He will be honored and loved on every hand. Now, that was an excellent disposition. But suppose when he heard that the man's harvest was going to be lost he had written a beautiful letter of condolence!

Suppose with all his college training and rhetorical discipline he had composed a poem and sent it to the old farmer, wishing him all manner of prosperity and even praying for it! Suppose he had done all that, he would have been like many of us Christians,—we have done the same thing toward God. God blessed us; we know it and feel it, and we are very thankful to-day,—so that we are ready to offer up our wordy thanksgiving,—but not the sacrifice!

How many persons now say "thank you," although some are so stingy in their words that they leave off the "you" and simply say "thanks"! But what is that in the sight of God but an unfruitful tree!

I was told last Wednesday night about a leading pastor of the country. He was born in Scotland, of poor parentage, and had but little opportunity to secure an education. He came to this country as a young man, and he was at work in a livery stable, trying to earn an honest living. He drove out to a small pond near New York with an old gentleman who ventured out on the ice to see the skaters. The ice gave way, and many of the skaters were precipitated into the cold water. The old gentleman was also overturned in the water and exposed to the dangers of death. The driver left his horse and waded as far as he could, and then, pushing aside the ice, swam out and saved this old gentleman, with two or three others. When he placed the man in the carriage, he wrapped him in his own overcoat and then he wrapped him in the robes, and drove hastily to a house nearby where the gentleman was acquainted. The saved man said, "What shall I give you?" The driver replied, "Nothing." The gentleman said, "What is your name?" "No matter," he replied, "I have only done my duty in the matter, and I don't want to be known. I am glad you are saved." He went back to the livery stable. It was more than two years after that when the old gentleman saw him again down at Castle Garden and recognized him as the youth that had saved him. He ran and called after him and said, "Won't you come to my house? I want to see you." He gave the young man his card, and, after considerable hesitation, the young man presented himself at the door and was ushered in by the servant. He was taken right into the open parlors and dining-room, in the midst of a great party. There were assembled the richest, the wealthiest, the most fashionable people of New York. The ladies were dressed in the completeness of fine drapery. Their eyes were bright, their cheeks flushed, their voices happy. The scene was fascinating, and completely overwhelmed the mind of the young man, who had never seen such bright lights and such flashing eyes. The daughter of the owner of the mansion said, "Who is that?" The servant said, "He is the one that your father sent for."

"Oh!" she said, "that is the young man that saved my father." She rushed forward to him in the midst of all that company, with all her array of fashionable attire and brilliant diamonds, and expressed to him her joy that she had found him. She brought him right up to the table and introduced him to the people, to his great dismay, terror and pain. "Certainly, bring him in here! Of course he is not dressed for a party, as he knew nothing of it, but bring him right in here and give him a seat at the table!" One of the wealthiest men of New York said, "You must have this place," and then went and asked the servant to bring in again the course that had already passed. At last, in his confusion, he managed to get out and he begged them to let him go. But this daughter of the millionaire bade him good-bye and said, "We will always be glad to see you. You will always be welcome in this house." Oh! how many a fashionable girl, even if all her relations would have been saved, would on a fashionable occasion like that have spurned to speak to the ordinary young man. But this daughter's gratitude went further. She asked her father to help that young man secure an education, and he obtained it. First he went to a preparatory school in New York, and then to Princeton University, and afterward he married the young lady, and they now live in a magnificent mansion, and last Wednesday night I was introduced to the family of this successful preacher, whose benefactions are so extensive and who has the assistance of that lovely and noble wife in all his work. I thought of that story, and thought how many thousands of young ladies there are who in the midst of their fashionable gatherings would have thought it a social disgrace to have welcomed any man not attired in a "dress suit." God makes a thousand human females to one real woman.

But it is just as true of churches as it is of individuals. I was interested yesterday in meeting the Methodist brethren in Baltimore as they assembled to consult over their missionary work. How many churches they have, as we have, in this country which, like the trees on my farm, grow up green and blossom, but they have no fruit. We gather so few final results. That is the history of our churches all over the land.

There is a man near Westfield, Mass., who, in memory of his father, keeps the old sawmill just as it was when his father died. The buzz saw is polished every day, and the dam is kept complete, and the gate is complete, and the wheel is repaired,— everything ready to run. It has been there I know not how long, but for quite a number of years, but it has not been through a single log in all those years, yet it has been polished and kept in complete condition to do the work it never does.

Like a woman who makes up dresses and never wears them, it is the disposition of the church to spend all its strength in *preparing* to do something. We have our prayer meetings. What for? What is the purpose? Jesus Christ said He came into this world to save the world, and the Apostle Paul, representing the highest aim of Christianity, said, "This is a faithful saying and worthy of all acceptation, that Jesus Christ came into the world to save sinners." That is the chief purpose of the church, and yet you will find churches in this country where they hold the prayer meeting for a whole year without one attempt to save anybody,—without a thought that they are there to save any soul. They come together and make their prayers and their short speeches, and prepare themselves for a work they never think of doing. It never occurs to them that it *can* be done!

How many societies we have in this church in which they are going through the same polishing of the saw; just the same repairing of the wheel; just the same keeping of the dam and reservoir in order! What is the Christian Endeavor Society for? It is to save sinners. That is the aim! That is the whole of it! But the Christian Endeavor Society says, "We wish to be trained in prayer, in Christian work." If the Christian Endeavor Society has been *preparing* itself for five years, why don't they do actual Christian work *now?* Why does it not gather some sinners? Why does it not go after some lost soul and thus bring forth the fruit for which it has been preparing? Why is not that the harvest of all the different societies in this church?

We have a great church! We have prepared this institution! We have gotten it ready for the great harvest, and the harvest is as fully prepared as we, yet we will go and hear Mr. Conwell preach, and the chorus sing, and then we will go home and think we have done the whole, when we are only just getting ready for work,—when we have only just come to the point where we can do something. We go out of this church with the idea that we wish to do better. Those of you who have witnessed this baptism this morning have a wish that you might reconsecrate yourselves to the Lord, and yet when you get out into the rain it will dampen the whole purpose, and you will come next Sunday the same. It has all been wasted, because you do not carry out the purpose for which Christ died and for which His church was instituted.

There was a man in Pennsylvania whom I always delighted to meet, who always found his way to his Thanksgiving dinner by the the way of his old mother's home. He took his mother something good and then went to his own Thanksgiving feast. Let no man who wants to serve God go to his Thanksgiving dinner this year without doing something for those whom Christ loves. It is the way to keep Thanksgiving. If a man this week, having in mind the hospital work for the good of those suffering poor for whom Christ died—if a man say, "I will do something for that hospital before I eat my Thanksgiving dinner," and do it, O! then he will make the "sacrifice of thanksgiving."

A man is not sincerely thankful until he is ready to make some positive sacrifice. Not far from here a man belonging to another church never eats his Thanksgiving dinner without hanging up a turkey in sight which he is going to give to somebody else. While it is a peculiar way of expressing it, it does express the great truth that I am trying to evolve this morning: that we, in order to be really thankful to God, need be thankful enough to express it in charitable deeds.

All who believe in the Lord Jesus Christ have everlasting life, but baptism is the test of that belief. If one believes in Jesus Christ enough to be baptized, then he is sure that he has believed enough to be saved. If a man is thankful enough to Christ for his blessings to his family so as to express it in some deed before his fellowmen, then he makes the true "sacrifice of thanksgiving"; then he goes to God with an offering that will be acceptable.

When Christ sat at that well at Samaria, waiting for His disciples to bring Him something to eat, a soul came that way. He came into the world to save souls, and when that woman of Samaria came, He talked with her until He was refreshed. He had meat to eat that they knew not of.

You can eat a Thanksgiving dinner for yourself after you have carried one to some poor people. Then you, too, can make your Thanksgiving dinner a spiritual feast. If you have made some one else happier or better in the name of Jesus Christ, you won't need all the luxuries heaped on your table. Christ talked to that soul at the well and pointed her to the Lord. Then He did not care for His dinner. It was of no more value to Him, because no feast could add to his exultant joy.

We ought to be thankful enough to bear fruit indeed. As a church we ought to be a saving people. As a society we ought to be a saving people. As individual Christians we ought to be saving souls. As lovers of God, and grateful for His goodness, we ought to worship Him by positive open sacrifice of something of value to us. The sacrifice should be real, practical, personal—the giving up of something for the good of some one else—and that "sacrifice of thanksgiving" will make your Thanksgiving Day the happiest you have ever seen, unless you have practiced this often before.

BENEDICTION

O Lord! we know that whether we have little or much ourselves on Thanksgiving Day, that it will be a very completely happy day if we have made some sacrifice for Thy sake, and for the sake of our fellowmen as an "offering of thanksgiving." O Jesus! inspire us with a sense of our obligation as sinners, to rise higher than mere words, into the realm of deeds, where we bring of the best of that which we love most, and sacrifice it gladly for Thy service, and as an expression of our obligation to Thee. Now may mercy and peace from God the Father, the Son and the Holy Spirit abide with us as through this week we try to make some distinct offering in His Name. Amen.

XV

A Christmas Thought

(MATTHEW VII:11)

IN the 7th chapter of Matthew and in the 11th
verse is the remark of the Saviour concerning
the goodness of God to man:

*"If ye then, being evil, know how to give good
gifts unto your children, how much more shall your
Father which is in heaven give good things to them
that ask Him?"*

This wonderful Book gives us information concerning a thousand things. Out of a single verse,
and out of this one verse, we get a great many suggestions of wisdom which apply to all conditions of
life. I select this remark of Christ, this illustration
of His, to show His interest and the interest of
God in the Christmas season—the season when
people have been in the habit of making presents one
to another, and to their families.

The time is now approaching when all people
think of the Christmas season. Whether they be
Jew or Gentile this season appeals to every heart.
It has its place in the economies of our business, its

place in our worship, its place in our home, and its approval in our conscience.

Jesus says: "If ye know how to give good gifts—." It requires remarkable wisdom to know that. It should have much more study than we have time to give to it if we studied until Christmas day. It is a season of mighty influence for good. It is a time when a man makes a great many friends, or loses them. It is a time of prosperity, or a time of loss. It is a decisive season just before the first of January. So important is the Christmas thought that it cannot be considered out of place for me to discuss it for a few minutes frankly and plainly.

If a man is going to give a Christmas present, his first thought should be whether he has the money or the property to make a suitable present. The Lord says unto us, "Owe no man anything." It meant, of course, in its spiritual interpretation that we are never to get in debt beyond our ability to pay. It does not say that we should not mortgage our houses. It does not say that we should not secure credit. Nothing of that is in the thought, but the thought, as the apostle expressed it, when you view it in connection with what precedes and what follows, is that we are not to go in debt where we have not the means to pay. That is the kind of owing that is condemned of the Scripture. If you should owe, before Christmas, more bills than you are able to pay, which are already due, you have no right to make a present at all. It is wrong, by the teaching of your conscience, as well as of the Bible, to give away other people's money. If all the money you hold is now due to some person, then you owe that, and you are commanded to "Owe no man anything."

Laying thus the cornerstone of my thought on that foundation, I would emphasize it by a different statement, but, in fact, a repetition. If a church is in debt for bills overdue more than it can now pay, it has no right to give away anything, not even to the poor. If a company in business owe more than the realization of their stocks and their securities would pay, it is a crime (it is counted so by the law of man, and it certainly is so by the law of God), for that firm to make a present of anything at Christmas time. If an individual finding himself in debt should give way to the temptation, for the pride that is in his soul, to take money that belongs to other people, and present it to his family, or present it to his acquaintance, he is using another man's money just as much as though he put his hand in his friend's pocket and stole it from his pocketbook. If a man were to buy an establishment worth a million dollars, and give a mortgage on it for five thousand dollars, that five thousand dollars is no debt. He has plenty with which to pay it, and that would in no wise interfere with his presents. But it is the owing of bills due that we cannot pay.

The importance of this may be emphasized by an illustration. A family years ago had only seven dollars for Christmas, for they were scrupulously out of debt. They had only seven dollars left, and they sat down together to discuss what they would do with that seven dollars, how to distribute it, how much could be invested for one, and how much for another; none were left unnoticed. If you have never sat down with only seven dollars for your Christmas and tried to decide how you would distribute that among a great many friends, you have lost one of the perplexities of human life. "How shall the seven dollars be invested so as to do the most good, please the greatest number of friends, and suit our own pride in the matter?" They laid out fifty cents in one place for one child, sixty cents for another, a dollar for another, then so much for grandmother, so much for an uncle, then a certain sum for a neighbor that had been very, very kind, and they came up to the last one cent. When only one penny was left, they said: "What will we do with that?" The greatest puzzle was what to do with that last cent. They said: "Let us send it to a friend living far away in a letter, and tell him that is all we have, that we have sent all there was left to him." The letter was sent, in a half facetious way, but it was taken in the most beautiful spirit. The man took that penny and invested it, reinvesting it, and kept on re-investing it, and it went on through the years. He, a bachelor, living in California, with delight watched the growth of that penny in his investments and speculations from one sum to another, until when the years had rolled around, the old home in the East was gone, the children were scattered, and the old folks were living with one of the daughters far away from the old homestead, there came news that the relative in California had died, and had left them the proceeds of that single penny. In his will he expressed his gratitude to them that they did not send him more, but that they sent him "all they had." The exact amount he left them I do not remember, and need not, for this illustration. But it was a very large fortune they had really gained from that penny. That gift of one cent was the best of all. It was the gift of a single penny, but it was given in that spirit, and with that motive which made it so powerful a gift at that precious Christmas season.

A young man was engaged to be married, and he desired very much to give his intended a diamond ring for an engagement ring. He had told his friends outside he was going to do that, and that he was going to get the money from an investment he had. But when he came to seek for his investment it was lost. Then he tried to borrow. He went to a friend, and told him he wished to borrow the money to buy this ring. His friend said to him: "Charles, take an old man's advice. Don't buy a diamond ring for your intended bride, but go to her like a man and tell her you did intend to do so, but that you have not the means to do it unless you borrow, and you are not willing to go in debt. Go tell her frankly, that that is your situation. If she would refuse you because of your poverty now, or because of your manly truthfulness, then she does not deserve you. You are better off without her. Go tell her like a man." The young man did go to the woman and told her he had lost what little investment he had, that he had lost it all. If she would be satisfied with one for a less amount he would buy it with his wages the next Saturday evening. What a noble thing that was to do, and how difficult for him—any man who has been engaged to be married, will understand. She appreciated his manly truthfulness. She loved him more, and respected him far more highly for the position he took. When he bought a little plain ring that cost so small a sum, she was more delighted than she could have been with a magnificent diamond. It taught him a great truth; it taught her a great truth.

A young man finding he could buy nothing of any especial value without going in debt, sat down and made a footstool evenings. He carved it as nicely as he could, put it together with great skill, and then took that to his intended bride as his Christmas present, and said: "This is of but little value, but I made it myself." It was only a few years ago that the man died. He left in connection with the investments for the libraries of New York over eight millions of dollars. At his funeral the old gray-haired bride brought out the old stool that he made as his first present to her. It looked so rude in all their rich surroundings, for on the wall there was a single picture that could have bought ten thousand footstools like that, yet all the years she had kept it treasured up as an evidence of his affection for her. Though he had given her diamonds, and had given her everything that riches could confer upon a loved woman, yet to her the dearest thing, and which she showed with the greatest affection when he had gone, was that simple footstool which he "made himself."

If we are to make a Christmas present, as Christ suggests, it should be given with a certain right motive. The motive is everything. If you make a present you should make it with a motive of conferring upon him a blessing, so that that present when it reaches him shall be a matter of inspiration, shall be a matter of instruction, or shall be to him an especial value, so that the person to whom you give shall be benefited by what you confer.

It is too plain, too simple to admit of much discussion, but it is so plain and so simple that very few of us ever follow the Christian plan. The Christian plan is to be of benefit to those who would help, and so we must study with care what we give.

You know that when they sent to the Indians some presents in the early days of the settlers the Indians sent back bundles of arrows, which indicated war, which was an insult to those who had communicated with them. It meant war, and such a present as that is an insult.

A man should send some part of himself; that is, something that is his own. You know that when that man wrote from the prison in France to his king, with the blood he had taken from his own veins in that celebrated letter, he said, "This is my heart's blood." Oh, how much that meant to the king. He had taken his own blood, something of himself, and put it into his letter. He should have sent at that time his love, as well as allegiance, and he did it all by putting in his own heart's blood. O to have something of yourself go with your present, something of your own taste, some of your own love. In our Bazaar in the lower halls there are handkerchiefs and other gifts sent by the wife of the President of the United States, and by Miss Crosby, the

sweet singer of Israel, now in her ninety-fourth
year, in Bridgeport, Conn. When we think of those
presents sent by distinguished individuals, of what
value are they? Intrinsically, of very little value,
and yet when you look upon them and the cards of
the people attached to them, you naturally think of
the person who sent them. Who sent them? When
we find that the great singer who had written so
many hymns for our hymn book, sent a gift, we
find she sent a suggestion of poetry, of age in its
glory and beauty, of the home of the angels so near
to her. On the other hand, from the White House
comes a handkerchief, and it suggests to us, the wife
of the President, and the President. So each article
is attached to the personality and associations of the
giver back of it. Because of their associations, there
is a vast difference in the good that they will do.
If you bought one of those handkerchiefs and made
it a Christmas present to a friend, you would send
an entirely different influence with one from what
you would have sent if you had sent the other.

When you visit a library given by Mr. Carnegie,
what do you think about that present to your community? It brings you what thoughts? Thoughts
of speculation, thoughts of working men who have
earned all that money, thoughts of the fact that he
has had far more than his share of this world's
goods. It brings you to the fact that he gives it,

and attaches his name to it. It brings you the thought that he is a man of the world who believes this world is all, and says he doesn't believe in the Bible, the Church or Christ. He told me he did not. That library brings you that thought every time you pass it if you know its history. Those books are valuable, the instruction they give is valuable, but are they also associated with such a giver? You can question the value of all such generosity, so-called, to the world because of its association with the giver. If George Washington had given it, or if some saintly man who had lived and sacrificed for the cause of humanity had given it, it might have a far different influence upon human character.

I use these illustrations only to show that a gift carries with it the character of the giver. You must be careful when you send a gift that you can send with it yourself, a noble, upright Christian character, a character that loves the things that are holy and righteous, a character that hates the things that are evil and wrong, a character that stands for the right always, and against evil always. You must send that with your present, or your present will be of little or no value.

A young lady may receive a present from a thief, or a libertine, or have it sent to her. If she knows from whom it comes, she indignantly sends it back, or hurls it into the street, because it is a damage to her to receive it. That is an extreme case, but every single person has something of that on one side or the other. Consequently, in giving your Christmas present, you are sending yourself whether you will or no with your present.

So then the first duty in giving a present is to have the heart right, and it illustrates the great gospel truth that at Christmas season God expects us to give something to Him. Our Heavenly Father expects us to make an offering—a gift to Him, and we sit down and take an account of stock to see what we can give. The only thing that is of any value to Him is our own personal identity—our soul. It is the only thing he cares for. All His entire valuation of a man is in his soul, and in that soul's character. If we are going to make a present to God, we must take an account of stock and see what kind of a present we can give Him, see if we can make it better, or if we can bring it in such a way that it will be more acceptable to Him. The great question in connection with our gifts is: What is our duty to our God? Christmas is coming, and when it comes let us make a present to the Almighty. The only thing we can give him is our own soul, and let us give Him those souls in such a condition, in such contrition for wrongdoing, in such a motive for doing future righteousness, that it will be acceptable to him. He will see a character coming with those

presents of contrition, a character of humble sub-
mission to His will, which will make it a beautiful
gift to God. On Christmas we give ourselves to
God.

There was a man living in southern California
a few years ago whose name I think was Louis
Westcott Beck. He had a little dog he called Rufus.
One day he was lost in the desert of southern California, one hundred miles from any habitation, in
that driving sand, where the mirrors of lakes deceive,
and where there is no water. It was the night before Christmas, and as he lay there on the sands
suffering so much for water he promised the Lord if
permitted to live to the next day, he would give himself to the Lord as a Christmas present. The next
day he was found by a traveler, and relieved, and he
kept his faith. If you had the *Youth's Companion*
I don't think you could read anything more interesting than the life of Westcott Beck and his dog
Rufus. That great desert has seen the bones of
thousands. Thousands of men, women and children have been lost on it, and have died of thirst,
and their bones have been found in the driving sand
for all these years since California was settled.
When going through that desert on the Southern
Pacific Railroad, you look far out upon the sand
and see the mirrored lakes, which are only an imi-

tation. There are no lakes there. The old lakes are all dried up. I was told that Mr. Beck, giving himself to God and humanity, asked on that Christmas day what he could do for God. What could he do? Then he thought how he would like to save other suffering people who had suffered as he had suffered. He give himself to God, and said: "I will do this humble thing, this one thing—devote my life to the saving of travelers across this desert. Now from day to day, and year to year, he goes over that desert setting guide-posts here and there, and sometimes leaving a little dried meat and food at a certain place, so that for the last four years not a single traveler has been lost upon that great desert, so far as is known, because Beck's guideposts can be found every mile or two over that hundred-mile stretch of desert. He and his dog have become the good Samaritans of southern California. He devoted himself to the Lord, and then he asked God what he should do, and concluded that was his task and devoted himself to that beautiful self-sacrificing work.

Christmas is coming to you and to me, and we are to give God a present. If we do, we will consecrate ourselves to some one branch of work on Christmas day, and not only try to bring Him a pure heart and a clean conscience, but also a determination that our lives shall be of greater value to Him than they have been in the past, so that we reach as a culmination to the Saviour's teaching here, not only how we should give Christmas presents to friends, but also how we should give ourselves as a present unto the living God.

THE END